Sew Drawstring Bags

Sew Drawstring Bags
First Published in 2025 by Zakka Workshop, a division of World Book Media, LLC

www.zakkaworkshop.com
134 Federal Street
Salem, MA 01970
info@zakkaworkshop.com

KINCHAKU POUCH TO BAG (LBS no.8156)

Originally published in Japanese language by Boutique-Sha, Tokyo, Japan
English language rights, translation & production by World Book Media LLC

Publisher: Satoru Shimura
Editors: Watanabe Eriko, Matsui Asami & Hitomi Takahashi
Proofreader: Kikuchi Erika
Photographer: Fujita Ritsuko
Styling: Bain Risa
Hair & makeup: Miwa Masako
Japanese book design: Koike Kayo
Pattern: Miyaji Mutsuko
Tracing: Sakakibara Yukari
English editor: Lindsay Fair
Translator: Namiji Singley

ISBN: 978-1-940552-94-1
Printed in China

10 9 8 7 6 5 4 3 2 1

Sew Drawstring Bags

14 Pretty Purses, Bags & Pouches in a Cinch

Introduction

This book features a variety of drawstring bag designs, from simple pouches perfect for beginners to more complex tote bags and purses featuring linings, gussets, and unique shapes.

The beauty of drawstrings bags lies in their versatility. They are convenient for organizing and storing small items that need to be accessed quickly and easily.

The designs in this book can be used to store cosmetics, jewelry, craft supplies, small toys, and gifts. They make wonderful presents for others, but are also a nice way to showcase your favorite fabrics and treat yourself to a special handmade item.

At the back of the book, you'll find a special threader tool that makes installing the drawstring cords a breeze, as well as some cotton cording that will work for a variety of designs in this book. Have fun exploring the wonderful world of drawstring bags and pouches!

Contents

Simple Drawstring *Pouch*

This style of drawstring closure creates a pretty ruffled shape at the top. You can personalize your bag with decorative labels, embroidery, and other embellishments.

Learn how to make a basic drawstring pouch, perfect for storing craft projects, toys, or gifts. Follow the step-by-step guide to learn how to sew the bag and lining, as well as how to insert a drawstring. These techniques will be used for projects throughout the book.

MATERIALS (for one pouch)

- **Outside fabric:** One fat quarter
- **Lining fabric:** One fat quarter
- **Cording:** 47" (120 cm) of 1/8" (4 mm) diameter rope
- **Label:** One 2 1/2" x 3" (6 x 7.5 cm) decorative label (optional)

Sew using 3/8" (1 cm) seam allowance, unless otherwise noted.

CONSTRUCTION STEPS

Cut the fabric

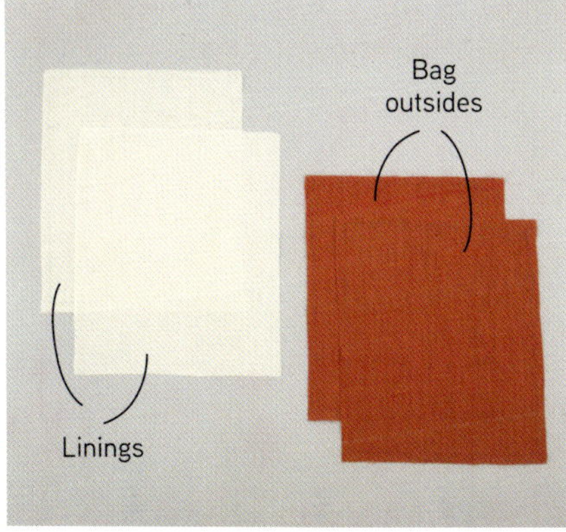

Use the template on Pattern Sheet A to cut 2 bag outsides and 2 linings.

Attach the label (optional)

Note: Blue thread is used in the photos for visual clarity. When selecting materials, use a thread color that matches your fabric.

Align the label on the right side of one bag outside (refer to the template for placement). Edgestitch the label in place, stitching 1/16" (2 mm) from the edge.

Sew the bag outside and lining together

1. Align one bag outside and lining with right sides together. Sew together along the top edge. Repeat with the remaining bag outside and lining to make two sets.

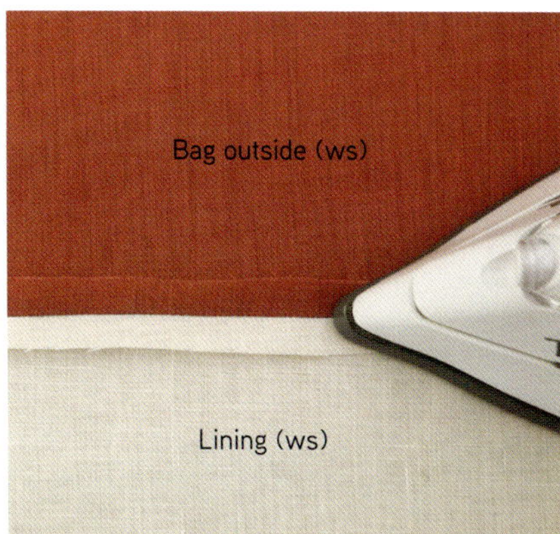

2. Press the seams open on both sets from step 1.

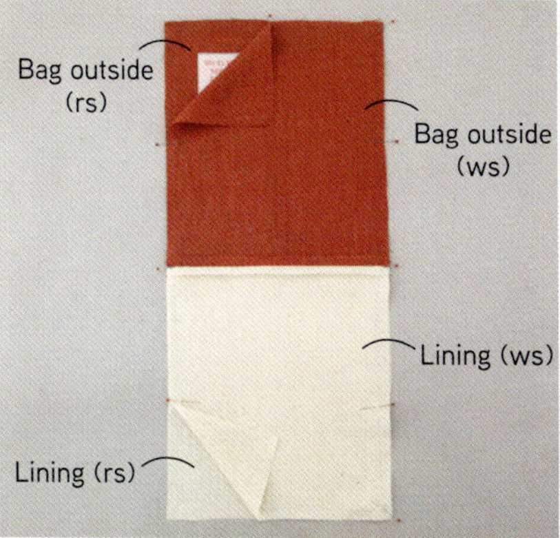

3. Align the two sets with right sides together so the two bag outsides are facing each other as are the two linings.

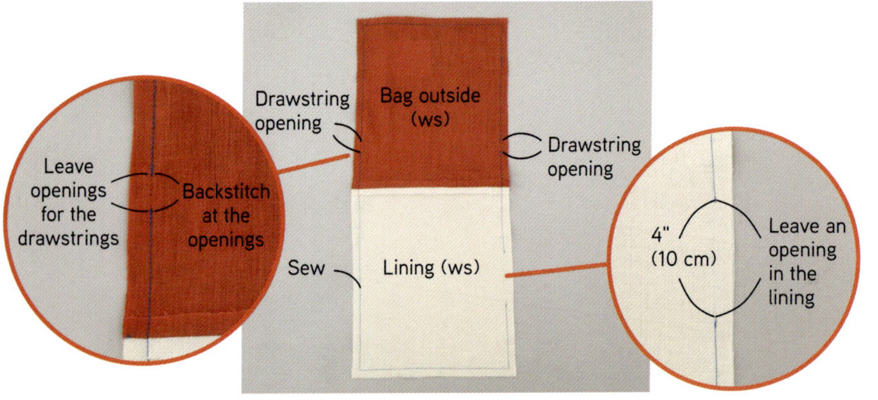

4. Sew together around the perimeter. Make sure to leave openings for the drawstrings on the bag outsides (refer to the template for placement) and a 4" (10 cm) opening in the lining. This will be used to turn the bag right side out.

5. Press the seams open.

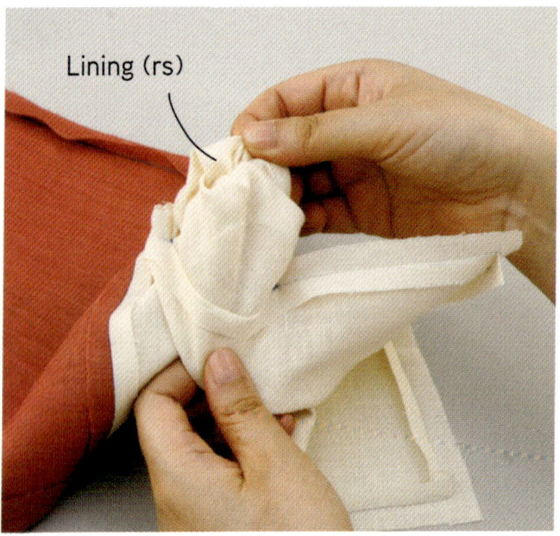

6. Pull the fabric through the opening in the lining to turn the bag right side out.

7. Adjust the shape and press with the iron.

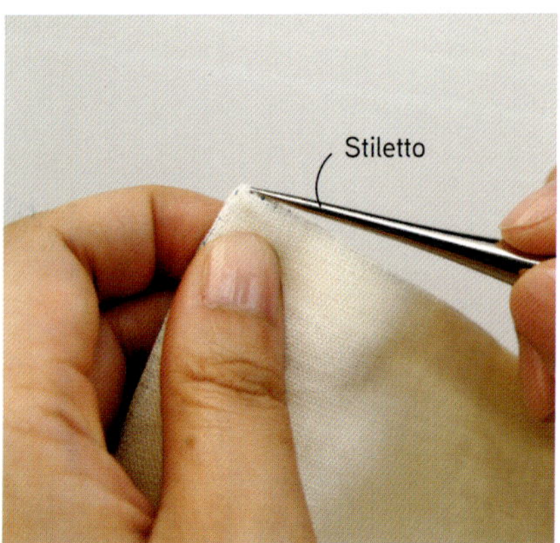

8. Use a stiletto to adjust the corners.

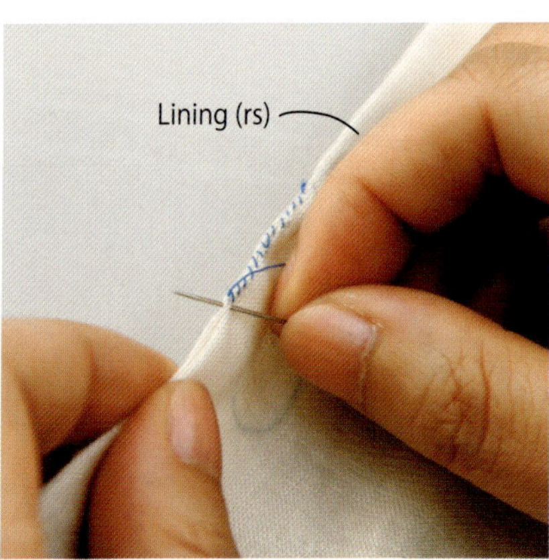

9. Hand stitch the opening in the lining closed.

Sew the drawstring casing

1. Tuck the lining inside the bag.

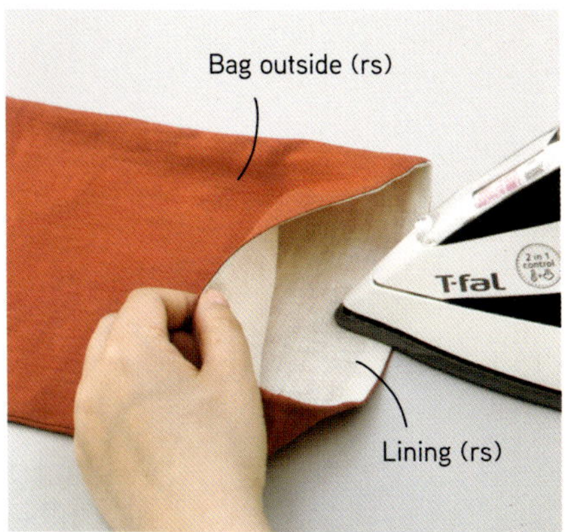

2. Adjust the shape and press with the iron.

To ensure a neat finish, use a water-soluble pen to mark the lines where you will topstitch. Make sure to test the pen on a scrap of fabric first to make sure that the lines will disappear with time or when the fabric is soaked in water.

3. Topstitch two rows of stitching to create the drawstring casing. Position the first row of stitching 2 ¼" (5.5 cm) from the top of the bag. Position the second row of stitching ⅝" (1.5 cm) beneath the first row.

Insert the drawstring using the threader tool

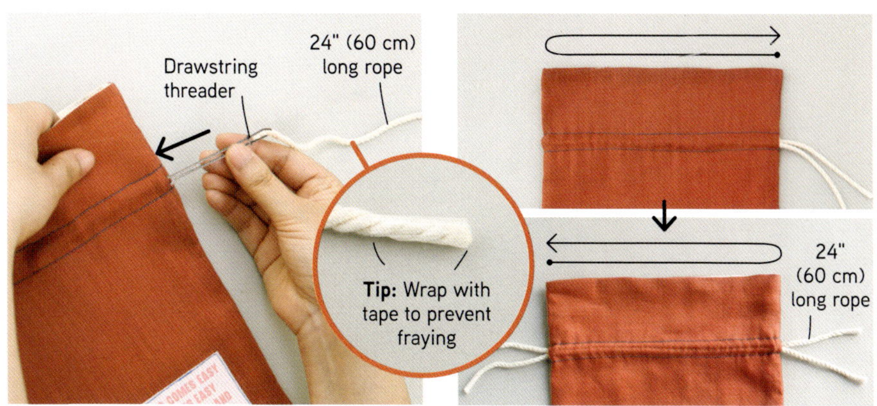

1. Insert one 24" (60 cm) long piece of rope through the drawstring casing using the drawstring threader tool included in the book.

2. Thread the cord through the drawstring casing on both sides of the bag, as indicated by the arrow in the top photo. Next, use the other opening to insert the other piece of cord through the drawstring casing in the opposite direction.

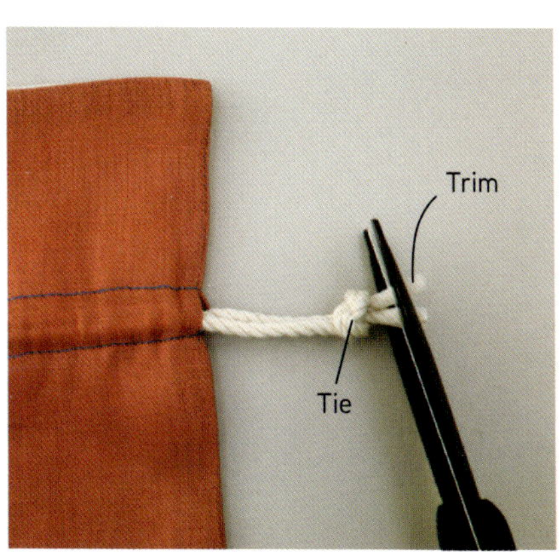

3. Tie the corresponding cord ends together and trim the excess (including the part wrapped in tape).

Finish

Ruffle Keepsake *Pouch*

This adorable drawstring pouch is designed to store jewelry, cosmetics, or other special treasures. With a pretty ruffle, it also makes a fun reusable gift bag.

MATERIALS

- **Outside fabric:** One fat eighth
- **Lining fabric:** One fat eighth
- **Ruffle fabric:** 1/8 yard
- **Cording:** 51" (130 cm) of 1/4" (6 mm) wide ribbon

CUTTING INSTRUCTIONS

Trace the templates on Pattern Sheet A. Cut out the following:

Outside fabric:

- 2 bag outsides

Lining fabric:

- 2 bag linings

Ruffle fabric:

- 1 ruffle

Sew using 3/8" (1 cm) seam allowance, unless otherwise noted.

CONSTRUCTION STEPS

Make the ruffle

a. Fold the ruffle in half with right sides facing out, creasing along the fold line marked on the template.

b. Baste along the curved edge, stitching through both layers of fabric. Sew two separate lines of basting stitches and leave long thread tails. Both lines of basting stitches should be positioned inside the seam allowance.

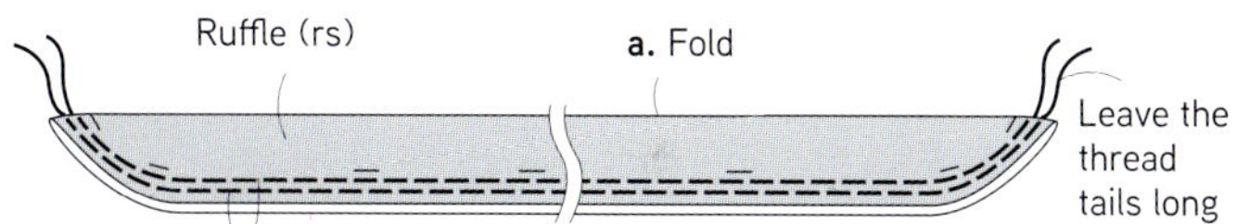

To baste, use a longer stitch length, generally a 4 or 5 on most sewing machines.

2. Attach the ruffle to the bag outside

a. Pull the thread tails to gather the ruffle fabric until its length aligns with the marks on the bag outside template.

b. Make sure the gathers are evenly distributed along the length of the ruffle. Pin the ruffle to one bag outside piece, aligning it with the placement marks noted on the template. Make sure that the basted edge of the ruffle is on the outside. Baste the ruffle in place, stitching inside the seam allowance.

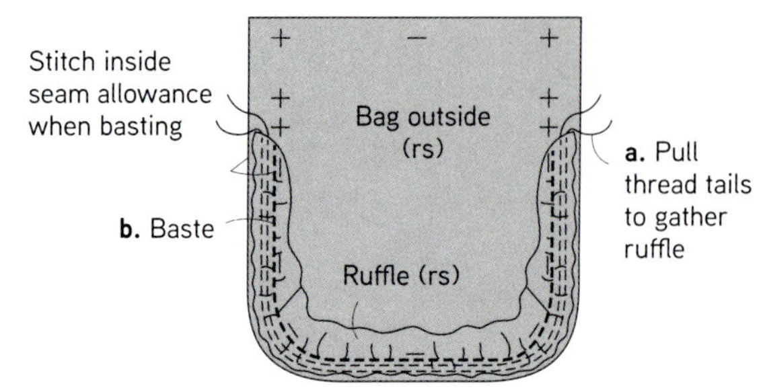

3. Sew the bag outside and lining together

a. Align the bag outside from step 2 and one lining piece with right sides together. Sew together along the straight edge.

b. Press the seam open.

c. Repeat steps a and b with the remaining bag outside and lining piece.

d. Open each set flat and align with right sides together so the two bag outsides are positioned face to face as are the two linings. Sew together around the perimeter, leaving the drawstring openings unsewn (refer to the template for placement). Also make sure to leave a 3" (7 cm) opening in the lining. This will be used to turn the bag right side out.

e. Make clips into the seam allowance along the curves, being careful not to cut through the stitching line. This will help create nice smooth corners and reduce bulk.

f. Press the seam open.

g. Turn the bag right side out through the opening in the lining.

h. Hand stitch the opening closed.

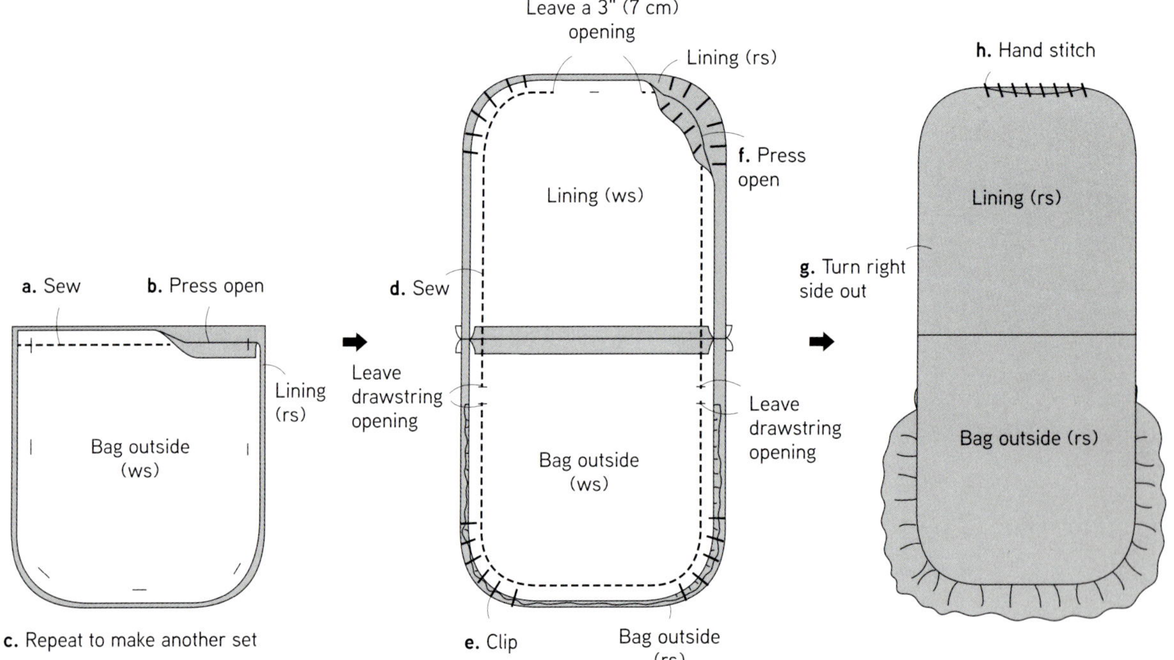

4. Make the drawstring casing

a. Tuck the lining inside the bag.

b. Topstitch two rows of stitching to create the drawstring casing. Position the first row of stitching 1 3/8" (3.5 cm) from the top of the bag. Position the second row of stitching 1/2" (1.3 cm) beneath the first row.

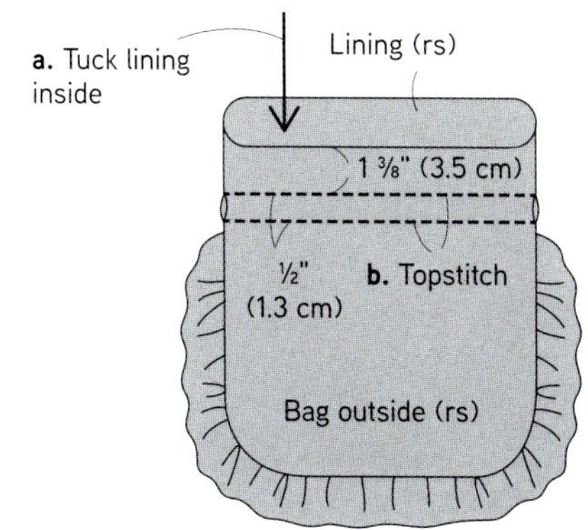

5. Insert the drawstrings

a. Pass a 25 1/2" (65 cm) long piece of cord through the casing using one of the drawstring openings.

b. Tie the two ends of the cord together in a knot.

c. Repeat steps a and b, inserting the cord through the other drawstring opening in the opposite direction.

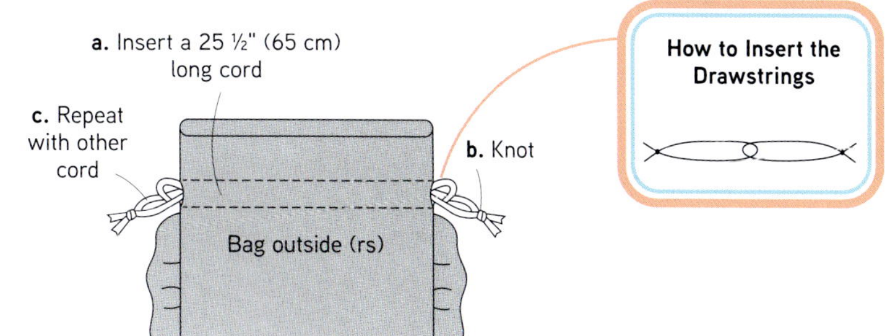

Finished Diagram

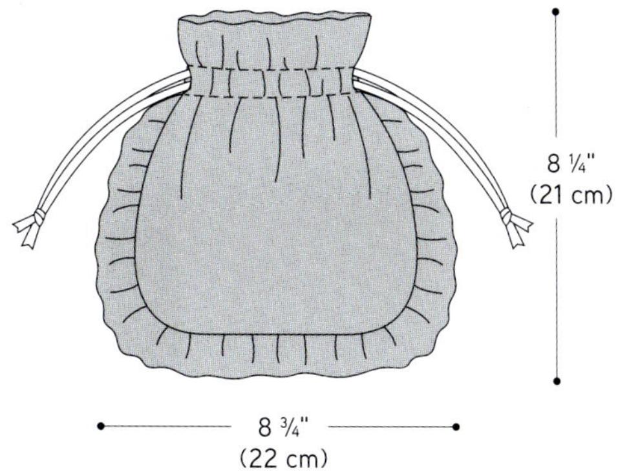

Small, Medium & Large
Oval Pouches

These cute oval pouches are handy for storing toys, gifts, and other odds and ends. This design comes in three different sizes and looks great as a set.

Try making all three sizes for a complete set!

Large

Medium

Small

MATERIALS (for one pouch)

- **Outside fabric:** One fat eighth
- **Lining fabric:** One fat eighth
- **Cording:** 1/8" (3 mm) diameter cotton cord
  - Small: 36" (90 cm)
  - Medium: 44" (110 cm)
  - Large: 48" (120 cm)

CUTTING INSTRUCTIONS

Trace the templates on Pattern Sheet A. Cut out the following:

Outside fabric:

- 2 bag outsides

Lining fabric:

- 2 bag linings

Sew using 3/8" (1 cm) seam allowance, unless otherwise noted.

CONSTRUCTION STEPS

1. Sew the bag outside and lining together

a. Align one bag outside and one lining piece with right sides together. Sew together along the straight edge. Repeat with the remaining bag outside and lining to make two sets.

b. Press the seam open on both sets.

c. Open each set flat and align with right sides together so the two bag outsides are positioned face to face as are the two linings. Sew together around the perimeter, leaving the drawstring openings unsewn (refer to the template for placement). Also make sure to leave a 2" (5 cm) opening in the lining. This will be used to turn the bag right side out.

d. Make clips into the seam allowance along the curves, being careful not to cut through the stitching line. This will help create nice smooth corners and reduce bulk.

e. Press the seam open.

f. Turn the bag right side out through the opening in the lining.

g. Hand stitch the opening closed.

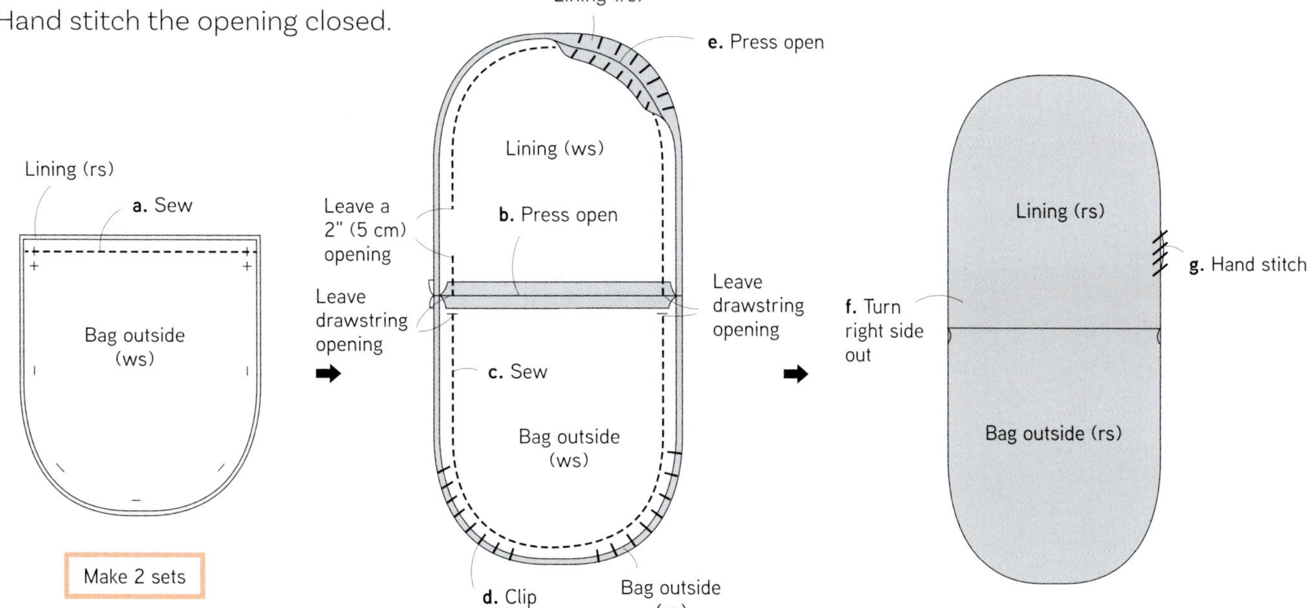

2. Make the drawstring casing

a. Tuck the lining inside the bag.

b. Topstitch a row of stitching ⅝" (1.5 cm) from the top of the bag to create the drawstring casing.

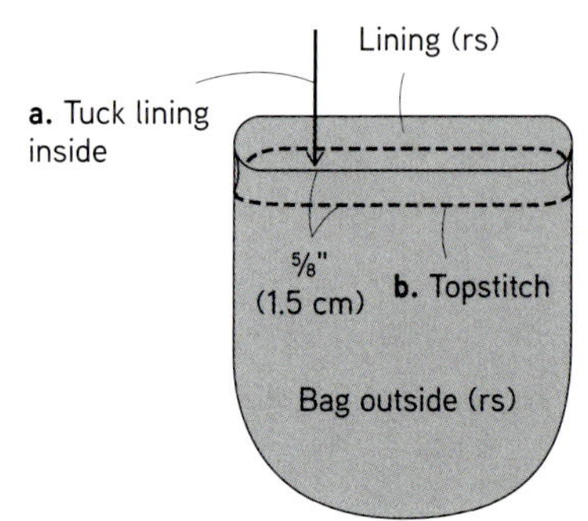

3. Insert the drawstrings

a. Pass a piece of cord through the casing using one of the drawstring openings. Refer to the chart below for cord length for each bag size.

b. Tie the two ends of the cord together in a knot.

c. Repeat steps a and b, inserting the cord through the other drawstring opening in the opposite direction.

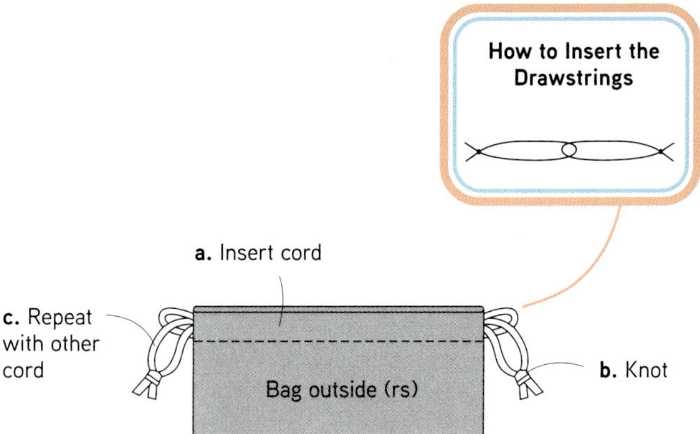

Bag Size	Cord Length (cut 2)
Small	18" (45 cm)
Medium	22" (55 cm)
Large	24" (60 cm)

Finished Diagram

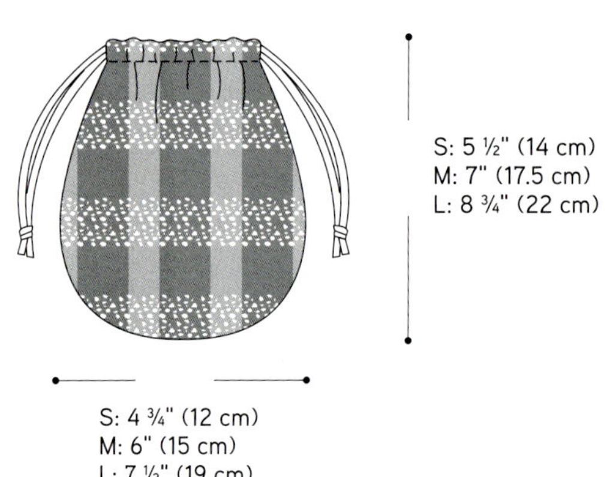

Animal Friends *Pouches*

You can't help but smile when you see these sweet bear and cat face pouches! They make great gifts for both little ones and animal lovers of all ages. These adorable samples were made with a solid cotton/linen blend fabric for the face and a gingham check for the ears, and then the facial features were embroidered with floss.

MATERIALS (for one pouch)

- **Outside fabric:** One fat eighth
- **Lining/ear fabric:** One fat quarter
- **Snout fabric (for the bear only):** 4" (10 cm) square
- **Cording:** 36" (90 cm) of 1/8" (4 mm) diameter cotton cord
- No. 25 embroidery floss in black, white and brown for the bear and dark brown, white, and light brown for the cat

CUTTING INSTRUCTIONS

Trace the templates on Pattern Sheet D. Cut out the following:

Outside fabric:

- 2 bag outsides

Lining/ear fabric:

- 2 bag linings
- 4 ears

Snout fabric (for the bear only):

- 1 snout

Sew using 3/8" (1 cm) seam allowance, unless otherwise noted.

CONSTRUCTION STEPS

1. Embroider the face

For the bear

a. Embroider the nose and mouth on the snout fabric, as noted on the template.

b. Use a needle and thread to baste long running stitches around the perimeter of the snout fabric. Make the stitches inside the seam allowance and leave long thread tails.

c. Cut the snout template out of a piece of cardstock (do not include seam allowance). Align the cardstock template with the wrong side of the snout fabric from step b.

d. Pull the thread tails to fold the seam allowance around the template.

e. Gently slide the cardstock out of the fabric. Knot the thread tails to secure the gathered fabric in place.

f. Hand stitch the snout to one of the bag outsides following the placement noted on the template.

g. Embroider the eyes as noted on the template.

Note: Use three strands of embroidery floss, unless otherwise noted.

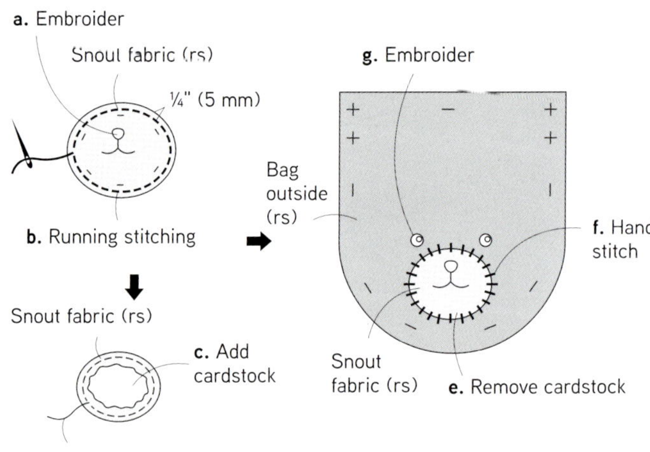

For the cat

Embroider the eyes, nose, mouth, and whiskers on one bag outside, as noted on the template.

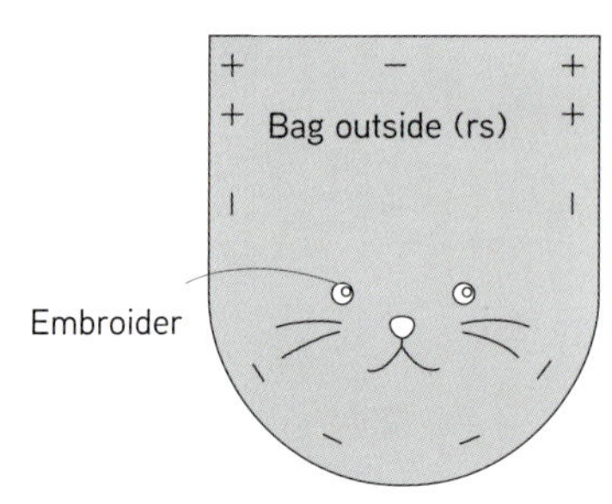

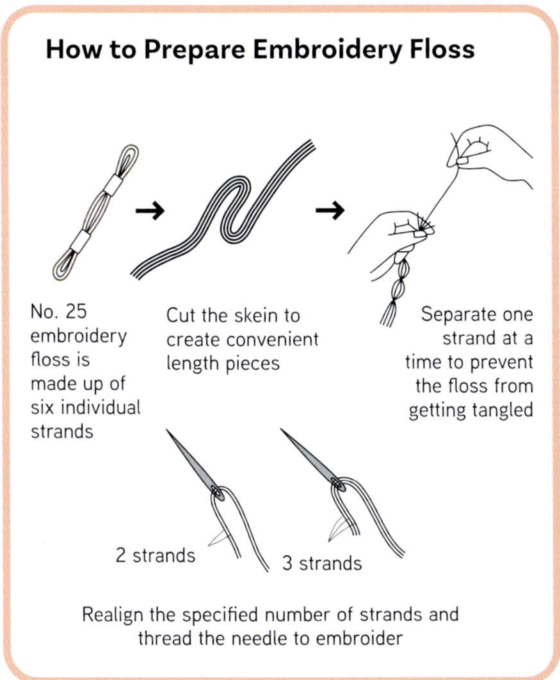

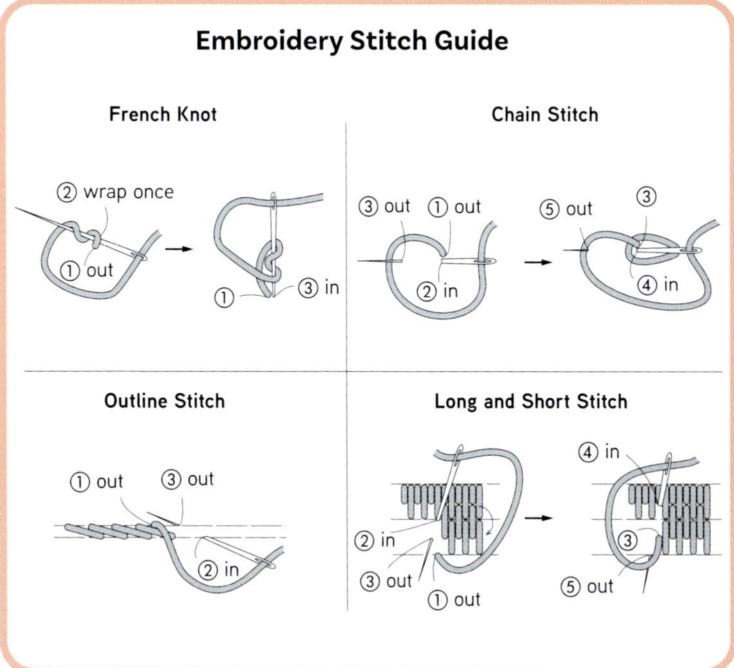

2. Make the ears

a. Align two ear pieces with right sides together. Sew, leaving the straight edge along the bottom open.

b. Trim the seam allowance to ¼" (5 mm).

c. Turn right side out.

d. Repeat steps a-c with the two remaining ear pieces.

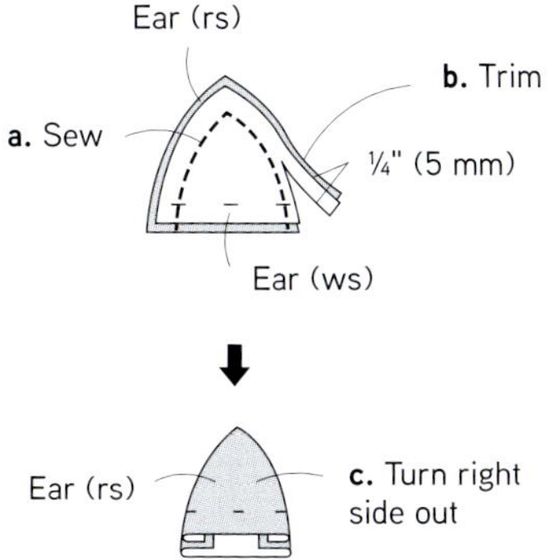

3. Attach the ears

Baste the ears to the embroidered bag outside following the placement noted on the template. Make sure to use ¼" (5 mm) seam allowance when basting.

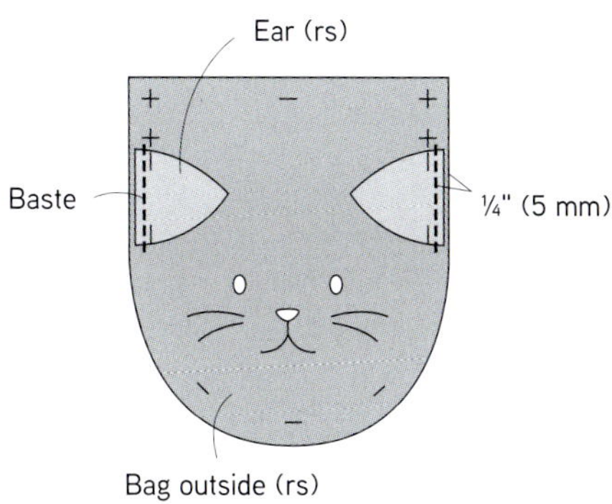

Sew the bag outside and lining together

a. Align one bag outside and one lining piece with right sides together. Sew together along the straight edge.

b. Press the seam open.

c. Repeat steps a and b with the remaining bag outside and lining piece.

d. Open each set flat and align with right sides together so the two bag outsides are positioned face to face as are the two linings. Sew together around the perimeter, leaving the drawstring openings unsewn (refer to the template for placement). Also make sure to leave a 2" (5 cm) opening in the lining. This will be used to turn the bag right side out.

e. Make clips into the seam allowance along the curves, being careful not to cut through the stitching line. This will help create nice smooth corners and reduce bulk.

f. Press the seam open.

g. Turn the bag right side out through the opening in the lining.

h. Hand stitch the opening closed.

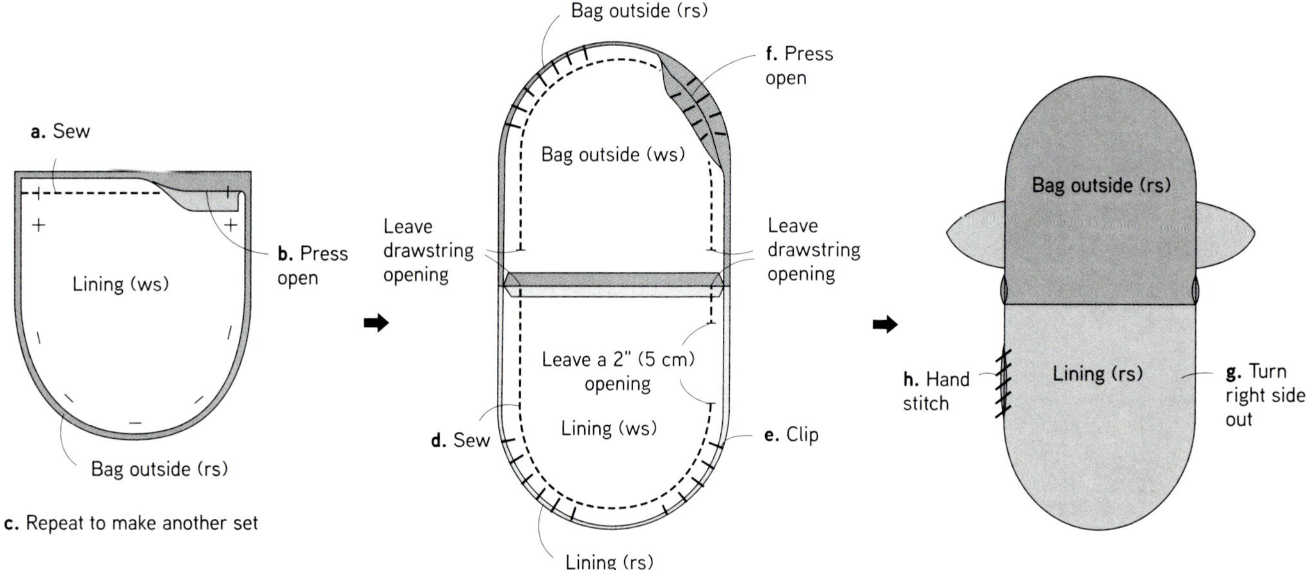

Make the drawstring casing

a. Tuck the lining inside the bag.

b. Topstitch a row of stitching 3/4" (1.8 cm) from the top of the bag to create the drawstring casing.

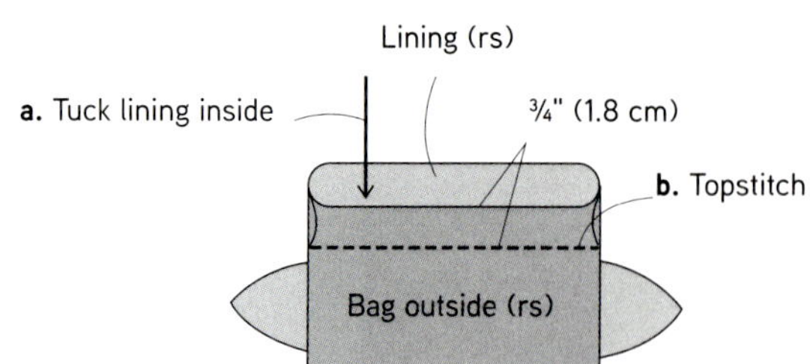

Insert the drawstrings

a. Pass an 18" (45 cm) long piece of cord through the casing using one of the drawstring openings.

b. Tie the two ends of the cord together in a knot.

c. Repeat steps a and b, inserting the cord through the other drawstring opening in the opposite direction.

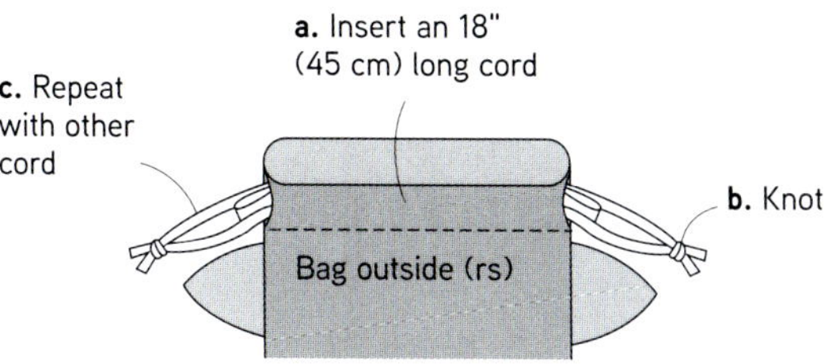

Finished Diagrams

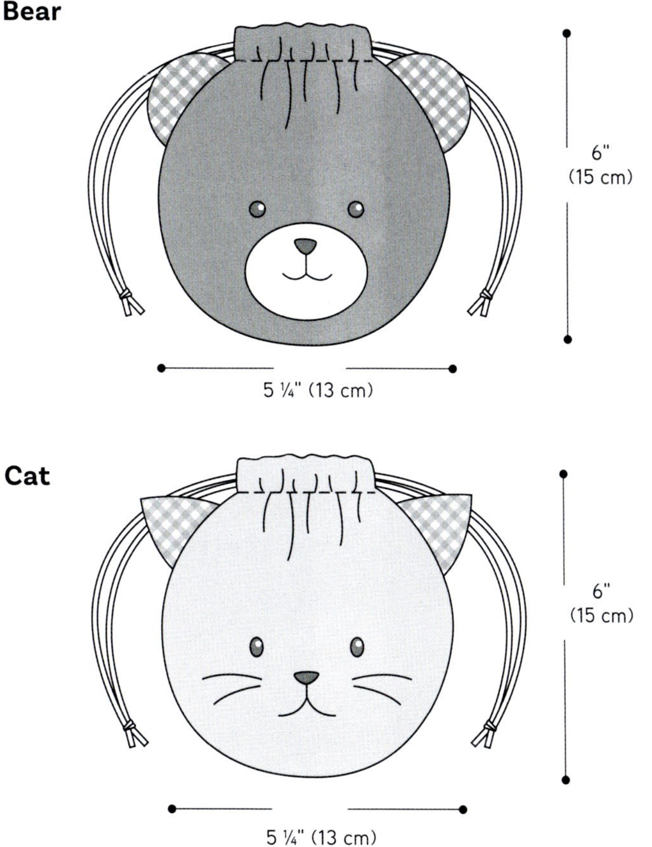

Fruit Drawstring *Pouches*

These sweet fruit-inspired pouches are sure to brighten anyone's day! With their dainty size, they are perfect for storing small toys, accessories, and games.

Pineapple *Pouch*

MATERIALS

- **Outside fabric:** One fat eighth
- **Lining fabric:** One fat eighth
- **Leaf fabric:** One fat eighth
- **Cording:** 48" (120 cm) of 1/8" (4 mm) diameter cotton cord

CUTTING INSTRUCTIONS

Trace the templates on Pattern Sheet B.
Cut out the following:

Outside fabric:

- 1 bag outside

Lining fabric:

- 1 bag lining

Leaf fabric:

- 4 leaves

Sew using 3/8" (1 cm) seam allowance, unless otherwise noted.

CONSTRUCTION STEPS

1. Make the bag outside and lining

a. Fold the bag outside in half with right sides together, creasing along the bottom fold. Sew together along the left and right edges.

b. Press the seams open.

c. Fold the lining in half with right sides together, creasing along the bottom fold. Sew together along the left and right edges, leaving a 2 1/2" (6 cm) opening in one seam. This will be used to turn the bag right side out.

d. Press the seams open.

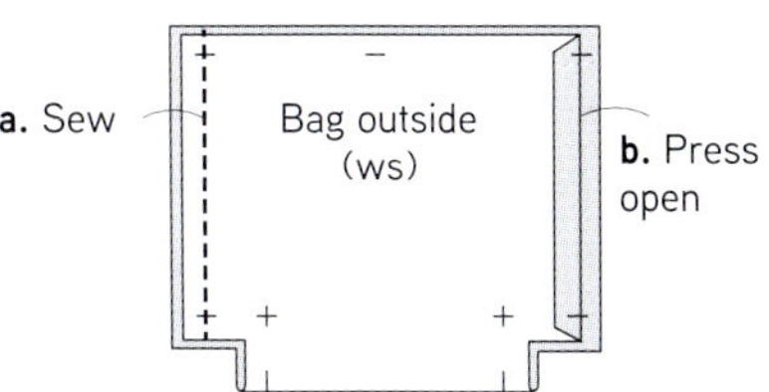

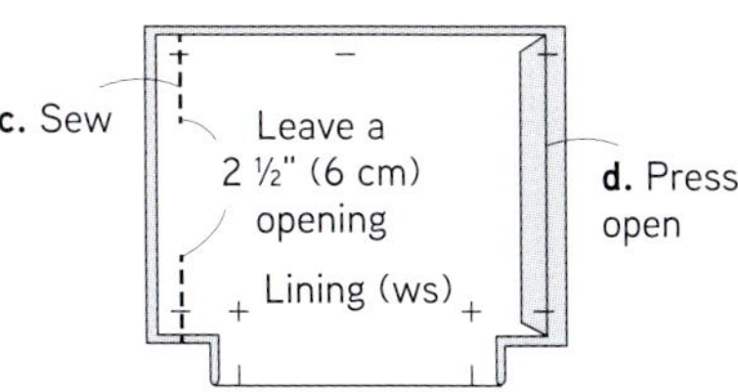

2. Miter the corners

a. On the bag outside, align each side seam with the bottom fold.

b. Sew a 2 1/2" (6 cm) long seam to miter each corner.

c. Follow the same process to miter the corners on the lining.

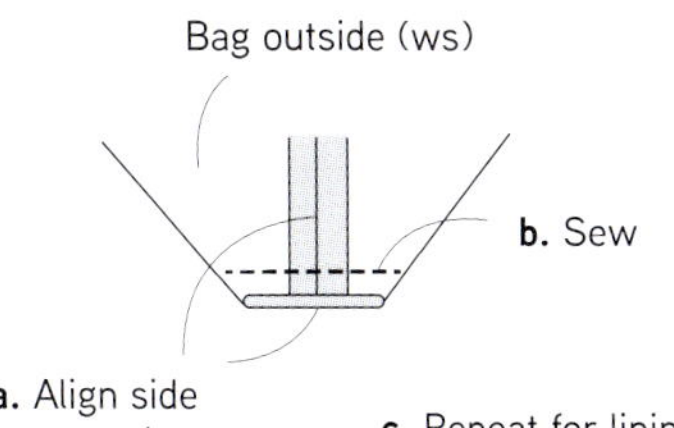

3. Make the leaves

a. Align two leaves with right sides together. Sew along the pointed edge, starting and stopping at the drawstring opening marks and leaving the straight edge open.

b. Trim the seam allowance to ¼" (5 mm).

c. Clip the points, creating V-shaped notches in the seam allowance. Make sure to leave about 1/16" (2 mm) of fabric from the point of the notch to the stitching.

d. Make clips into the seam allowance along the valley portions of the leaves.

e. Press the seams open.

f. Turn right side out.

g. Fold and press the seam allowances under along the left and right edges, in the area beneath the drawstring openings. Edgestitch in place, stitching as close to the fold as possible.

h. Repeat steps a–g with the two remaining leaves.

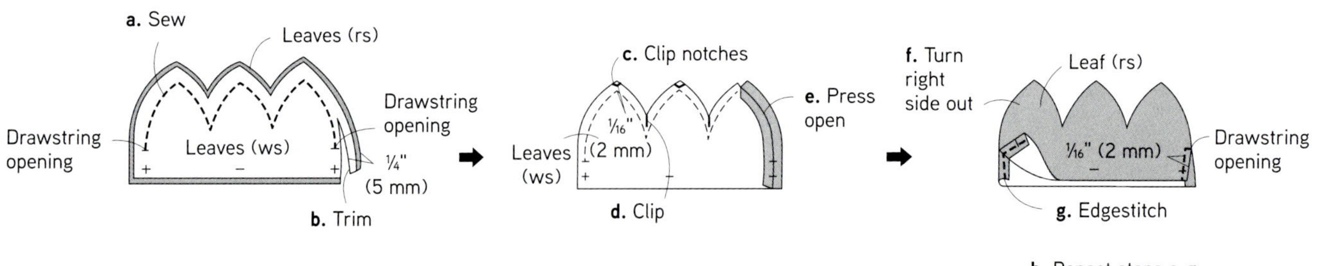

4. Attach the leaves

Align the two leaves with the bag outside with right sides together, matching the straight edges of the leaves up with the top edge of the bag outside. Baste in place using ¼" (5 mm) seam allowance.

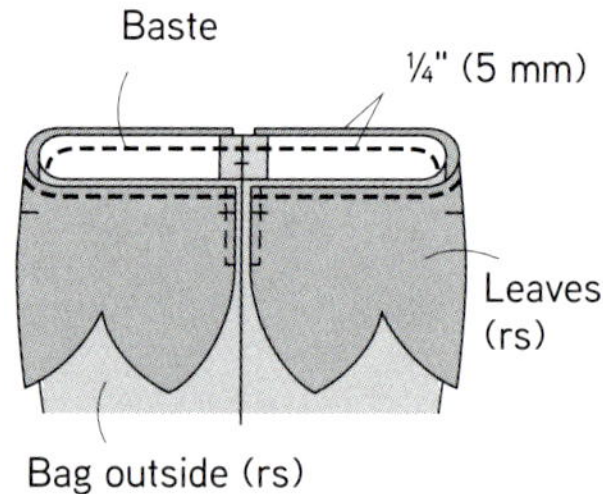

5. Sew the bag outside and lining together

a. Insert the bag outside into the lining with right sides together.

b. Sew together around the top of the bag.

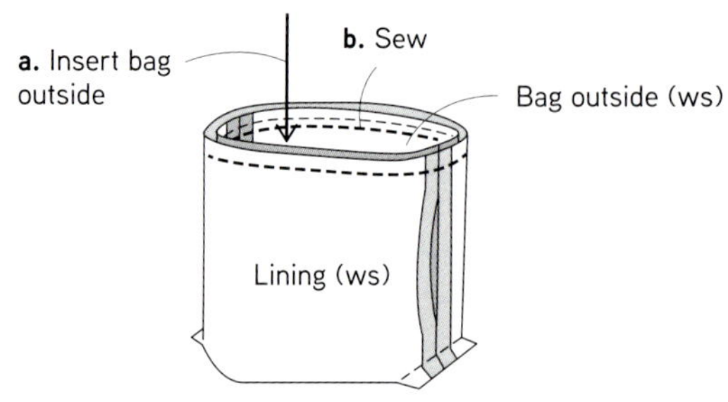

6. Sew the drawstring casing

a. Turn the bag right side out, but leave the lining separate from the bag outside.

b. Hand stitch the opening in the lining closed.

c. Tuck the bag outside into the lining. Edgestitch the lining, stitching just below the seam where the leaves meet the lining.

d. Topstitch another row of stiching ⅝" (1.5 cm) above the row sewn in step c.

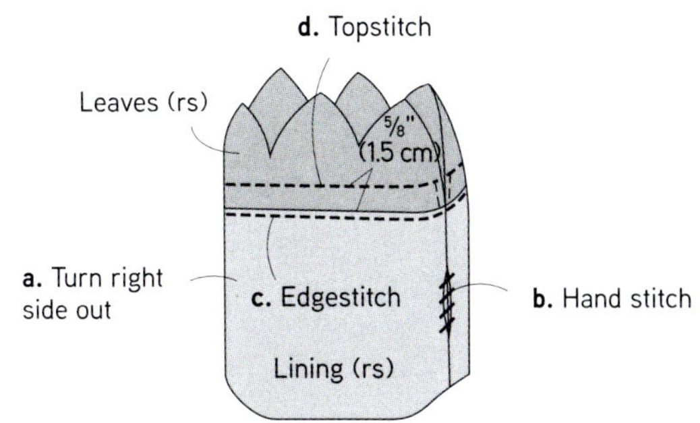

7. Insert the drawstrings

a. Pass a 24" (60 cm) long piece of cord through the casing using one of the drawstring openings.

b. Tie the two ends of the cord together in a knot.

c. Repeat steps a and b, inserting the cord through the other drawstring opening in the opposite direction.

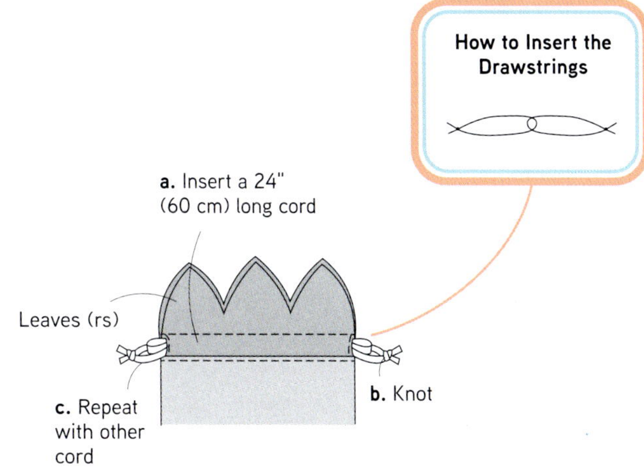

Finished Diagram

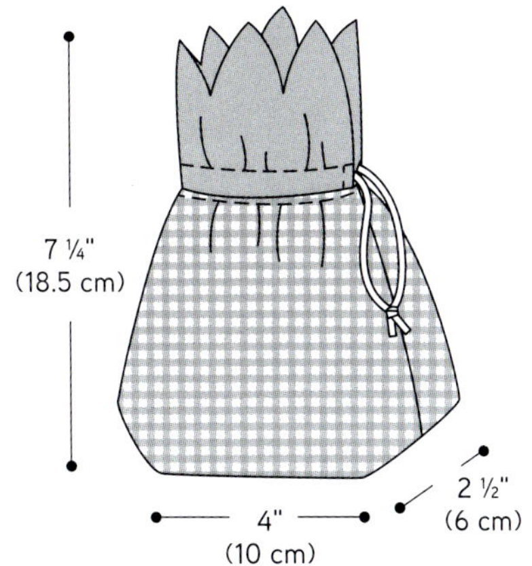

Strawberry Pouch

MATERIALS

- **Outside fabric:** One fat eighth
- **Lining fabric:** One fat eighth
- **Leaf fabric:** One fat eighth
- **Cording:** 44" (110 cm) of 1/8" (4 mm) diameter cotton cord

CUTTING INSTRUCTIONS

Trace the templates on Pattern Sheet B. Cut out the following:

Outside fabric:

- 2 bag outsides

Lining fabric:

- 2 bag linings

Leaf fabric:

- 2 small leaves
- 2 large leaves

Sew using 3/8" (1 cm) seam allowance, unless otherwise noted.

CONSTRUCTION STEPS

1. Make the bag outside and lining

a. Align the two bag outsides with right sides together. Sew together around the curved edges, leaving the straight top edge open.

b. Clip the point, creating a V-shaped notch in the seam allowance. Make sure to leave about 1/16" (2 mm) of fabric from the point of the notch to the stitching.

c. Press the seam open.

d. Repeat steps a-c to make the lining.

e. Insert the lining into the bag outside with right sides facing out.

f. Baste around the top of the bag using 1/4" (5 mm) seam allowance.

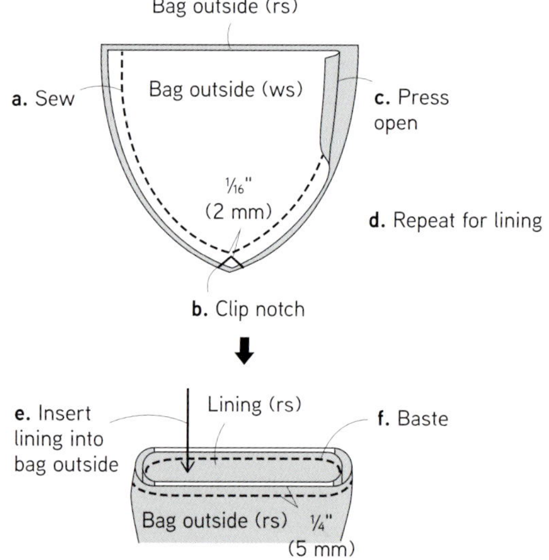

2. Make the leaves

a. Align a large and small leaf with right sides together, matching up along the pointed edge. Sew together along the pointed edge, starting and stopping at the raw edge of the small leaf and leaving the straight edge open.

b. Trim the seam allowance to 1/4" (5 mm).

c. Make clips into the seam allowance along the valley portions of the leaves.

d. Clip the points, creating V-shaped notches in the seam allowance. Make sure to leave about 1/16" (2 mm) of fabric from the point of the notch to the stitching.

e. Press the seams open.

f. Turn right side out.

g. Repeat steps a–f with the two remaining leaves.

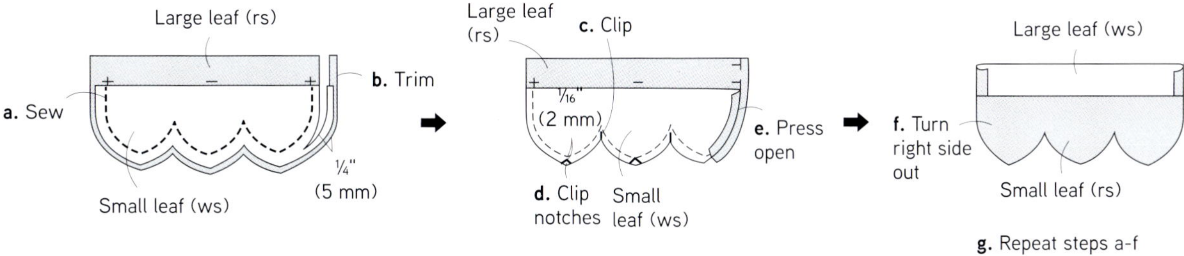

3. Attach the leaves and sew the drawstring casing

a. Align a large leaf with the lining with right sides together, matching the straight edge of the leaf up with the top edge of the lining. Pin in place. Fold the leaf to the outside of the bag. Topstitch ½" (1.3 cm) from the top of the bag to create the drawstring casing.

b. Repeat process with the remaining leaf.

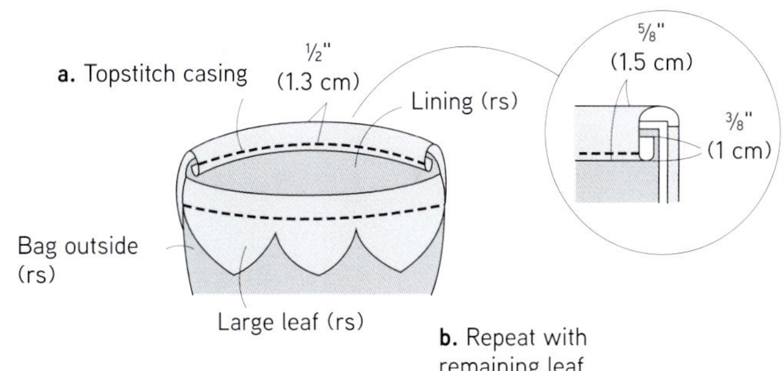

4. Insert the drawstrings

a. Pass a 24" (60 cm) long piece of cord through the casing using one of the drawstring openings.

b. Tie the two ends of the cord together in a knot.

c. Repeat steps a and b, inserting the cord through the other drawstring opening in the opposite direction.

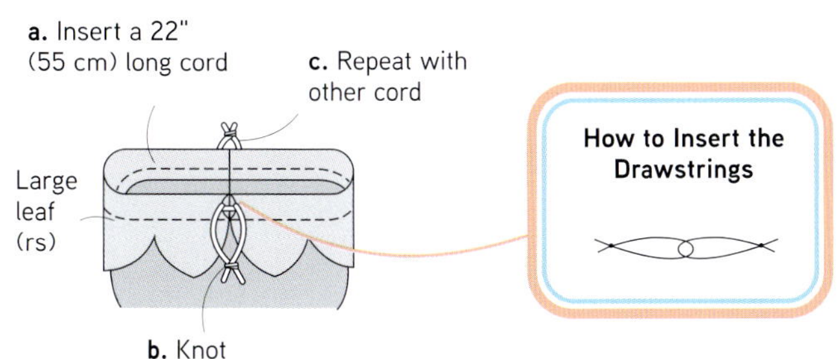

Finished Diagram

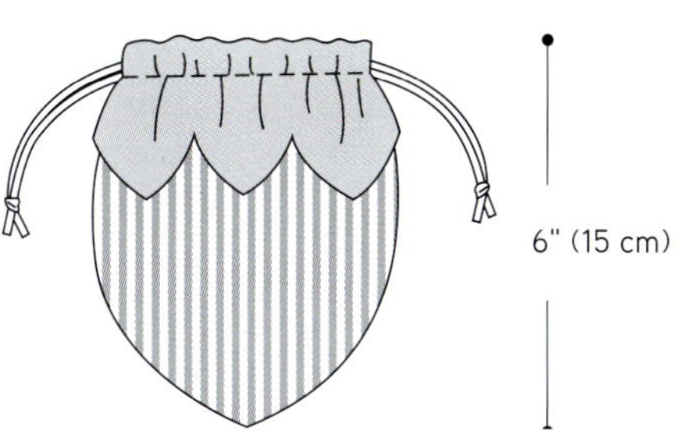

Gusset *Pouches*

With their cute round shape, these pouches are perfect for combining different fabrics. Version B features two drawstrings with cord locks on each side of the bag, while version A has a single drawstring and cord lock.

Use fusible fleece to give the bag a soft, rounded shape.

A

B

Designed by: Sentir le vent (Kazuyo Tsurumi)

MATERIALS (for one pouch)

- **Outside fabric:** One fat eighth
- **Gusset fabric:** One fat eighth
- **Lining fabric:** One fat quarter
- **Fusible interfacing:** 4" x 16" (10 x 40 cm)
- **Fusible fleece:** 31 1/2" x 16" (80 x 40 cm)

For Version A

- **Cording:** 24" (60 cm) of 1/8" (3 mm) diameter waxed cotton cord
- One cord lock
- Four 1/4" (5 mm) inner diameter grommets

For Version B

- **Cording:** 44" (110 cm) of 1/8" (3 mm) diameter waxed cotton cord
- Two cord locks
- Four 1/4" (5 mm) inner diameter grommets

CUTTING INSTRUCTIONS

Trace the templates on Pattern Sheet B. Cut out the following:

Outside fabric:

- 2 bag outsides

Gusset fabric:

- 1 gusset

Lining fabric:

- 2 bag linings
- 1 gusset lining

Fusible fleece:

- 2 bag outsides
- 2 bag linings
- 1 gusset

Fusible interfacing:

- 1 gusset lining

Sew using 3/8" (1 cm) seam allowance, unless otherwise noted.

CONSTRUCTION STEPS

1. Make the bag outside

a. Adhere fusible fleece to the wrong side of both bag outsides and the gusset.

b. Sew the bag outsides to the gusset with right sides together, starting and stopping at the gusset seam allowance. **Note:** Make sure to align the gusset with the bag outsides following ✶ marks noted on the template. The gusset will not extend to the edges of the bag outsides.

c. Make clips into the seam allowance along the curved areas.

d. Press the seams open.

e. Turn right side out.

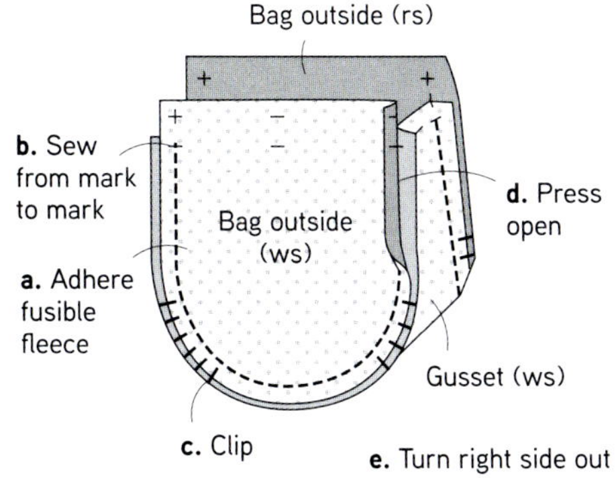

2. Make the bag lining

a. Adhere fusible fleece to the wrong side of both bag linings.

b. Adhere fusible interfacing to the wrong side of the gusset lining.

c. Sew the bag linings to the gusset lining with right sides together, starting and stopping at the gusset seam allowance, not at the edge of the fabric.

d. Make clips into the seam allowance along the curved areas.

e. Press the seams open.

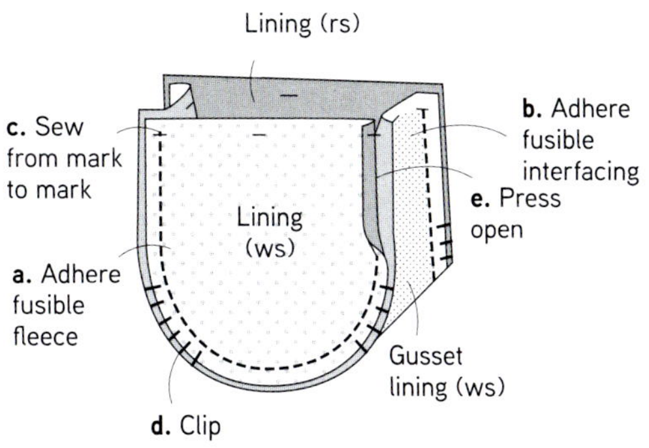

3. Sew the bag outside and lining together

a. Insert the bag outside into the assembled lining with right sides together.

b. Sew together at the top of the gussets only.

c. Turn the bag right side out but position the lining on the outside of the bag.

d. Baste together at the top using ¼" (5 mm) seam allowance.

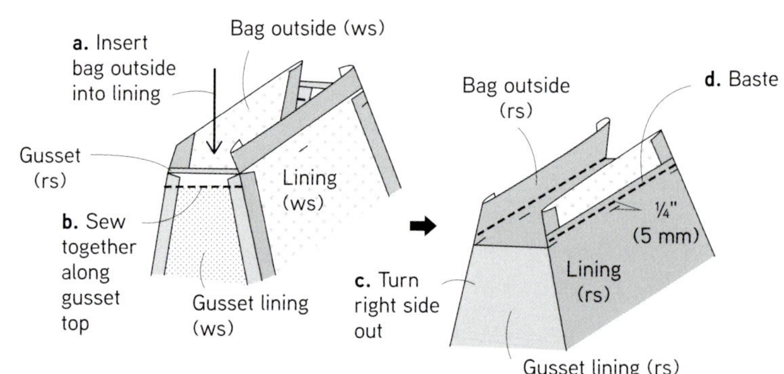

Make the drawstring casing

a. Fold and press the seam allowance to the wrong side on the portions of the bag outsides that extend at the top. Next, fold this portion down so it overlaps the lining (refer to template for placement).

b. Hand stitch to secure the folded fabric to the lining. This will serve as the drawstring casing for the bag.

c. Install the grommets following the placement noted on the template.

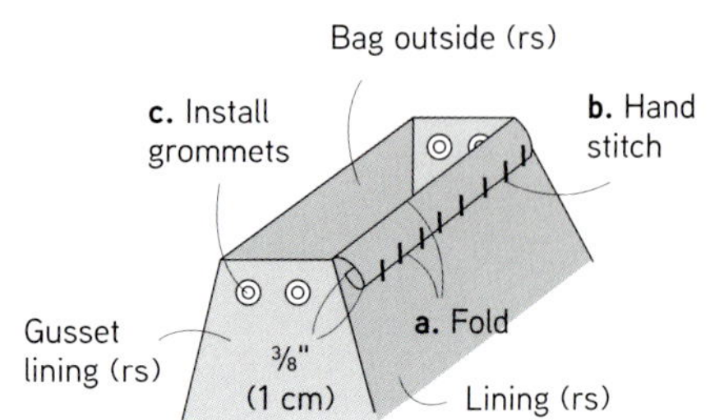

Insert the drawstrings

a. Pass a 22" (55 cm) long piece of cord through one set of grommets and then through the casing. Next, insert the cord ends through the remaining set of grommets.

b. Insert the cord ends through a cord lock and then tie the ends together in a knot.

c. For version B only, repeat steps a and b, inserting the cord through the grommets and casing in the opposite direction.

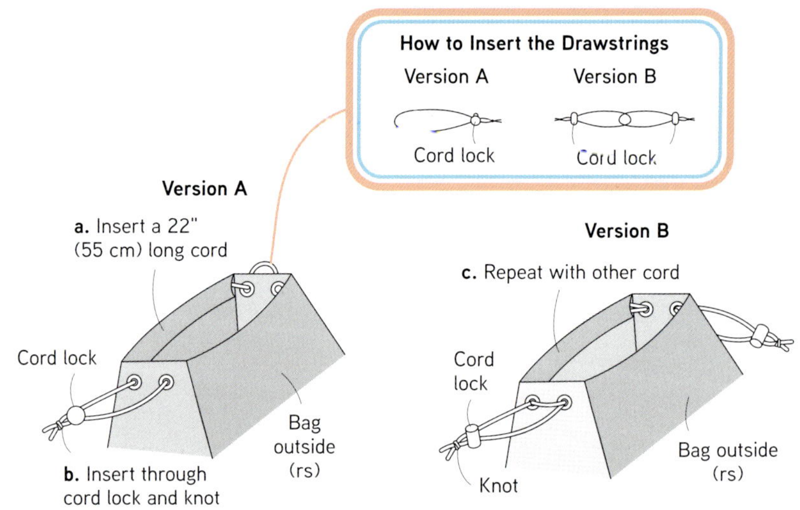

How to Use Cord Locks

1. Wrap the two ends together with tape

2. Press on the end to open the hole

3. Insert the cords through the hole

4. Tie a knot

To adjust, press on the end to open the hole and move the stopper up and down the length of the cords.

Finished Diagrams

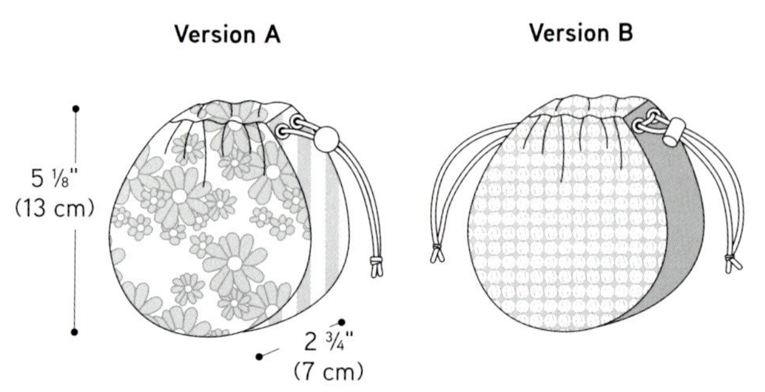

Floral Appliqué *Purse*

A scrappy appliqué flower lends this simple drawstring pouch a charming handmade feel. Add a shoulder strap to convert the pouch into a functional crossbody bag.

A pocket on the back offers extra storage.

This bag features a variety of special details, such as a colorful appliqué flower, hand quilting, and twill tape drawstrings finished with buttons.

Designed by: Sentir le vent (Kazuyo Tsurumi)

MATERIALS

- **Outside fabric:** 1/3 yard
- **Pocket fabric:** One fat eighth
- **Lining fabric:** One fat quarter
- **Patchwork fabric:** 4" (10 cm) squares of 7-8 different prints
- **Fusible fleece:** 31 1/2" x 16" (80 x 40 cm)
- **Tape for D-ring tabs:** 4" (10 cm) of 3/8" (1 cm) wide tape
- **Tape for drawstring:** 51 1/4" (130 cm) of 5/8" (1.6 cm) wide cotton twill tape
- Four 3/4" (2 cm) diameter buttons
- One 1/2" (1.2 cm) diameter plastic snap set
- Two 3/8" (1 cm) inner diameter D-rings
- One 3/4" (2 cm) wide shoulder strap (Zakka Workshop Item #ZW6783)

CUTTING INSTRUCTIONS

Trace the templates on Pattern Sheet C. Cut out the following:

Outside fabric:

- 2 bag outside A
- 2 bag outside B

Pocket fabric:

- 1 pocket

Lining fabric:

- 2 linings

Patchwork fabric:

- 12 petals
- 1 flower center
- 14 casing patchwork pieces

Sew using 3/8" (1 cm) seam allowance, unless otherwise noted.

CONSTRUCTION STEPS

Make the appliqué flower motif

a. Align two petals with right sides together and sew from mark to mark. **Note:** Sew the petals together using 1/4" (7 mm) seam allowance.

b. Press the seam to one side.

c. Follow the same process to sew all 12 petals together.

d. Baste along the curve of each petal, using 1/8" (3 mm) seam allowance. Leave long thread tails.

e. Make a cardstock petal template (do not include seam allowance). Align the template with the wrong side of a fabric petal. Pull the thread tails to gather the curved seam allowance around the template. Press with the iron, then carefully remove the template and repeat the process for the remaining 11 petals.

f. Baste around the flower center using 1/8" (3 mm) seam allowance. Leave long thread tails. Make a cardstock flower center template (do not include seam allowance). Align the template with the wrong side of the fabric flower center.

g. Pull the thread tails to gather the curved seam allowance around the cardstock template. Press with the iron, then carefully remove the template.

h. Hand stitch the petals to the right side of one bag outside A (refer to template for placement).

i. Hand stitch the flower center in place (refer to template for placement).

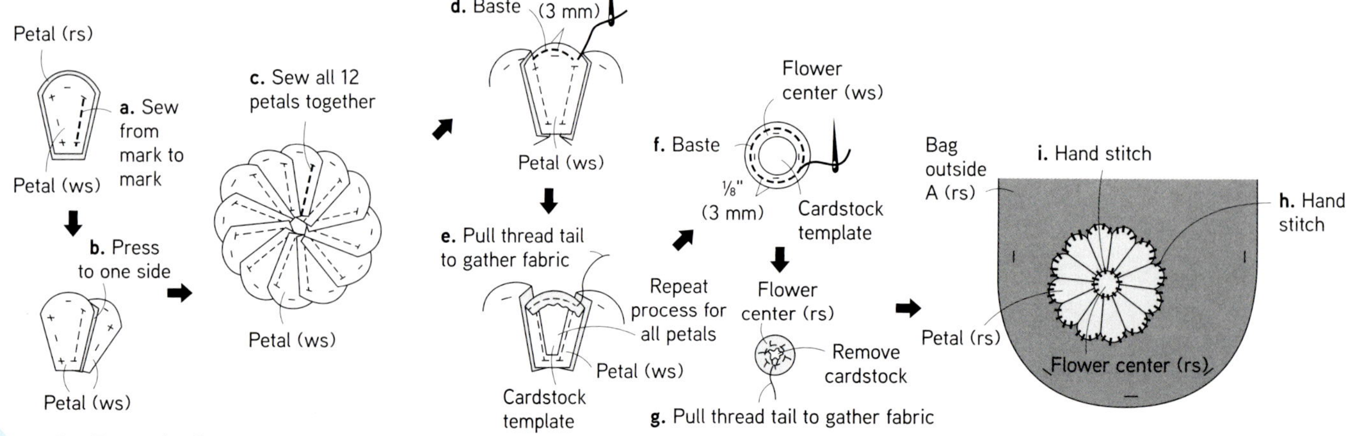

Make the patchwork for the drawstring casings

a. Align two casing patchwork pieces with right sides together and sew along one edge. **Note:** Sew the petals together using ¼" (7 mm) seam allowance.

b. Press the seam toward one side.

c. Follow the same process to sew a total of seven patchwork pieces together, then make another set of seven.

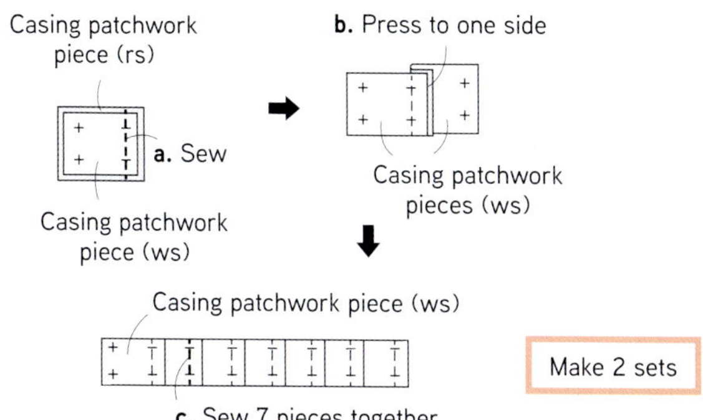

Assemble the bag outsides

a. Align one assembled drawstring casing with the straight edge of one bag outside A with right sides together and sew.

b. Press the seam toward bag outside A.

c. Next, align one bag outside B with the remaining free edge of the drawstring casing with right sides together. Sew, then press the seam toward bag outside B.

d. Repeat steps a–c to make another bag outside.

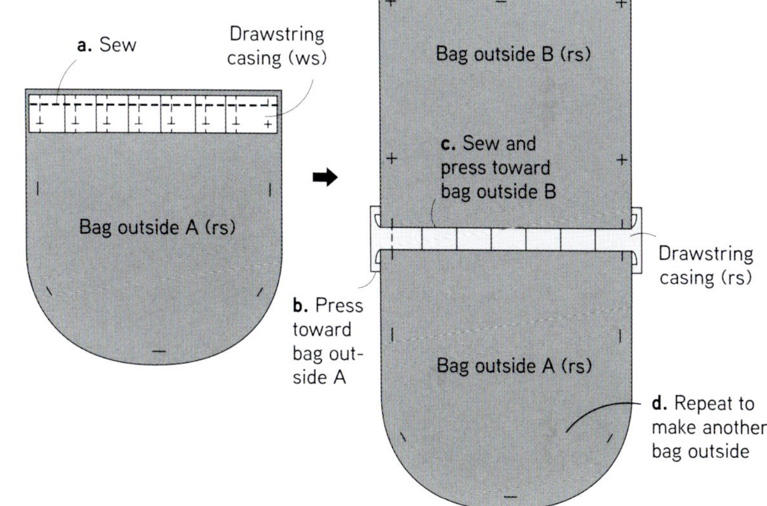

4. Quilt the bag outsides

a. Cut a piece of fusible fleece that covers the area beneath the marked fold line. Adhere fusible fleece to the wrong side of the bag front (the bag outside with the appliqué flower).

b. Quilt the portion of the front beneath the drawstring casing with diagonal grid lines spaced ³/₄" (2 cm) apart. Take care to avoid the appliqué flower.

c. Topstitch each patchwork piece in the drawstring casing, stitching as close to the seam as possible.

d. Topstitch each petal, stitching as close to the seam as possible.

e. Repeat steps a–c to quilt the remaining bag outside.

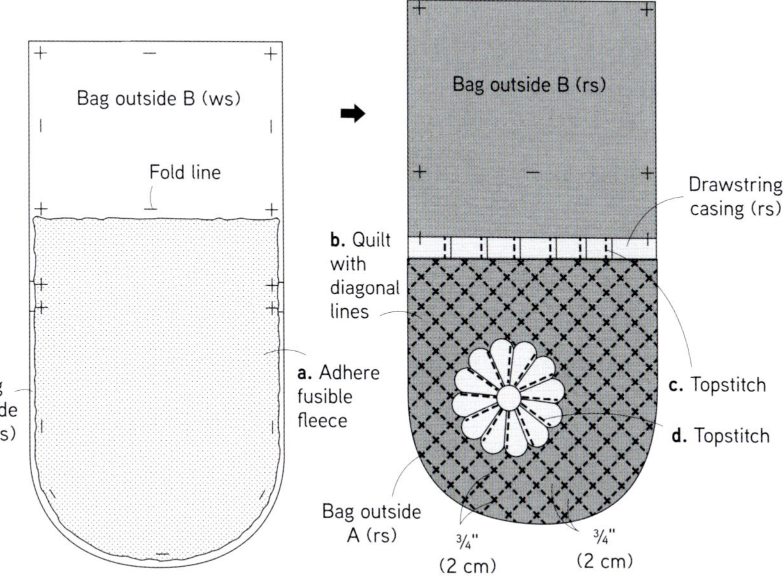

5. Make the pocket and attach it to the bag back

a. Cut a piece of fusible fleece that covers the bottom half of the pocket, just shy of fold line (refer to template for placement). Adhere fusible fleece to the wrong side of the pocket.

b. Fold the pocket in half along the marked line.

c. Quilt with horizontal lines spaced 5/8" (1.5 cm) apart. The horizontal quilting lines should start 1/4" (5 mm) from the folded edge.

d. Install the plastic snap on the pocket and bag outside (refer to templates for placement).

e. Align the pocket with the bag back, matching the pieces up along the bottom curve. Baste in place using 1/4" (5 mm) seam allowance.

f. Thread a D-ring onto a 1 1/8" (3 cm) long piece of 3/8" (1 cm) wide tape. Fold the tape in half.

g. Baste the folded tape to the right side of bag outside B using 1/4" (5 mm) seam allowance (refer to template for placement).

h. Repeat steps f and g to make and attach another D-ring tab.

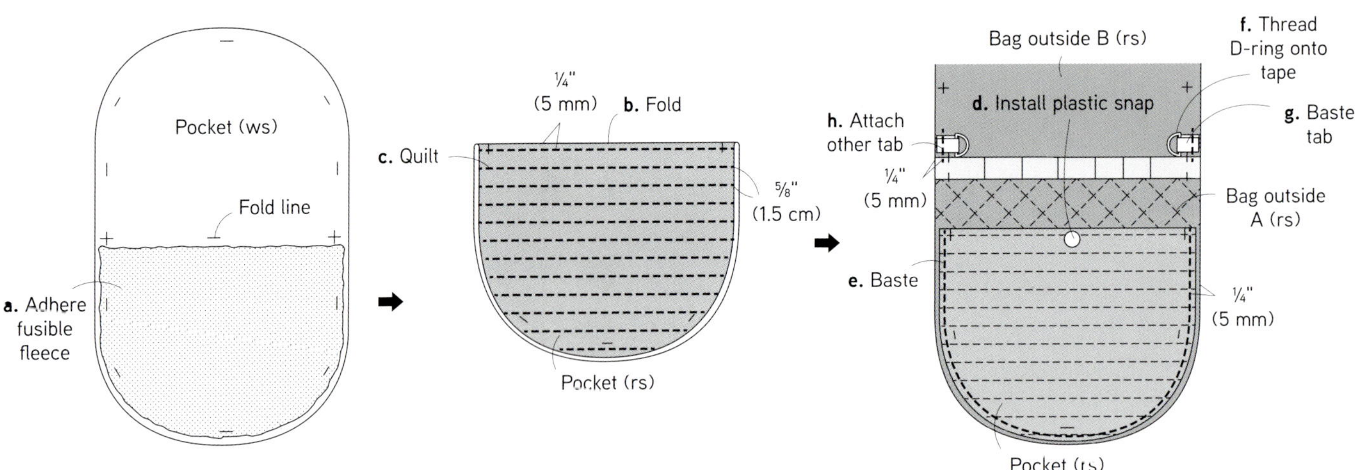

6. Sew the front and back together

a. Align the front and back with right sides together. Sew together around the curve, leaving two 3/4" (2 cm) openings for the drawstrings (the openings should start and stop at the top and bottom edges of the drawstring casings).

b. Press the seam open.

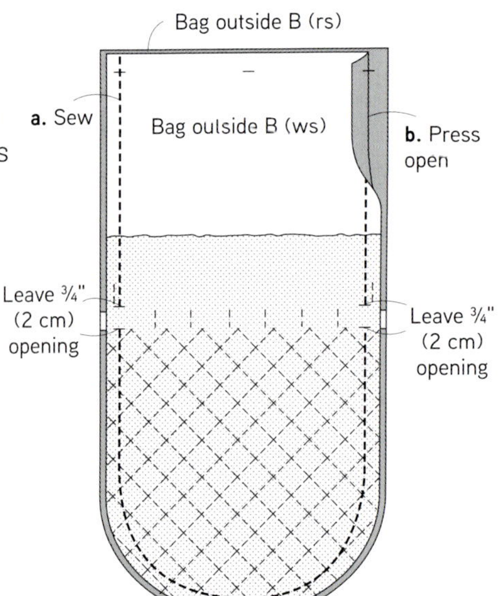

7. Make the lining

a. Align the two lining pieces with right sides together and sew together around the curve.

b. Press the seam open.

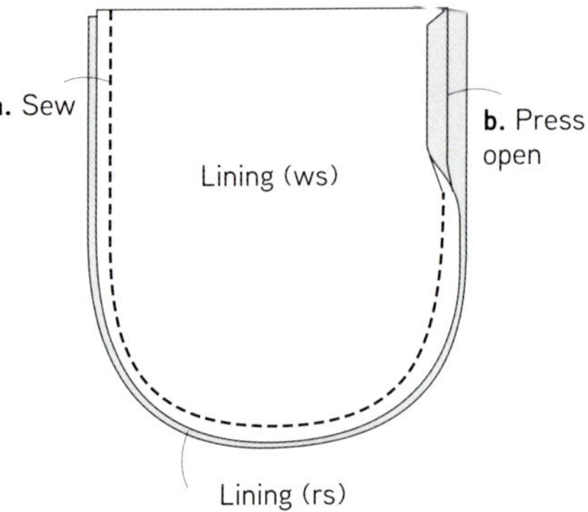

8. Attach the bag outside and lining

a. Fold and press the top straight edge of the bag outside over 3/8" (1 cm) to the wrong side.

b. Insert the bag outside into the lining with wrong sides together.

c. Fold the bag outside along the marked line (refer to template). Part of bag outside B will now form a facing on the inside of the bag.

d. Hand stitch the folded edge from step a to the lining. **Note:** The bag outside fabric will overlap the lining fabric.

e. Topstitch two rows of stitching along the top of the bag. Position one row of stitching 1/4" (5 mm) from the edge and the other row as close to the edge as possible.

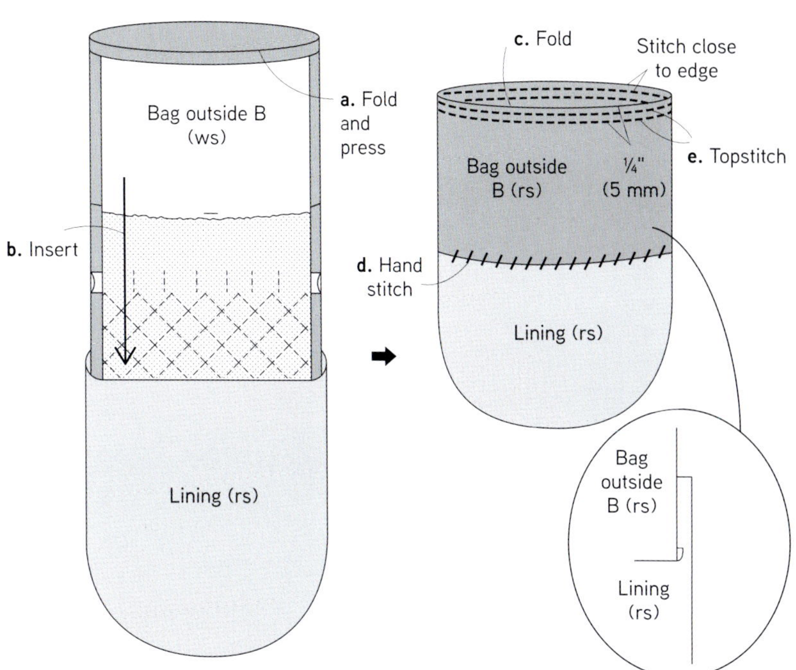

9. Topstitch the drawstring casing

Topstitch the drawstring casing, stitching as close to the top and bottom edges of the casing as possible. **Note:** The stitching will go through the lining as well, but take care to topstitch the front and back of the bag separately.

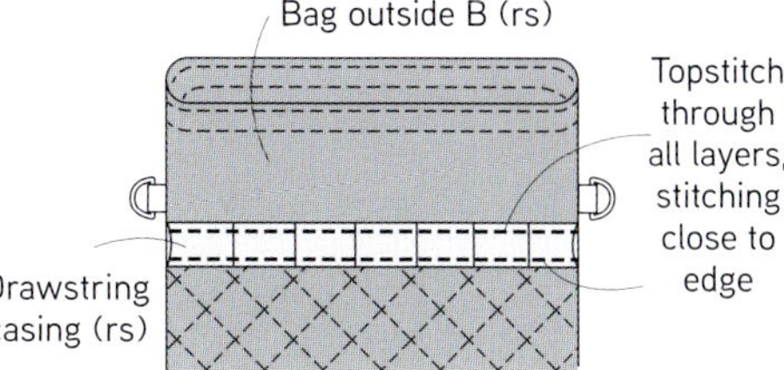

10. Insert the drawstrings

a. Pass a 26" (65 cm) long piece of twill tape through the casing using one of the drawstring openings. Repeat, inserting another 26" (65 cm) long piece of twill tape through the other drawstring opening in the opposite direction.

b. Sandwich corresponding twill tape ends between two buttons and sew, stitching through both the twill tape and buttons.

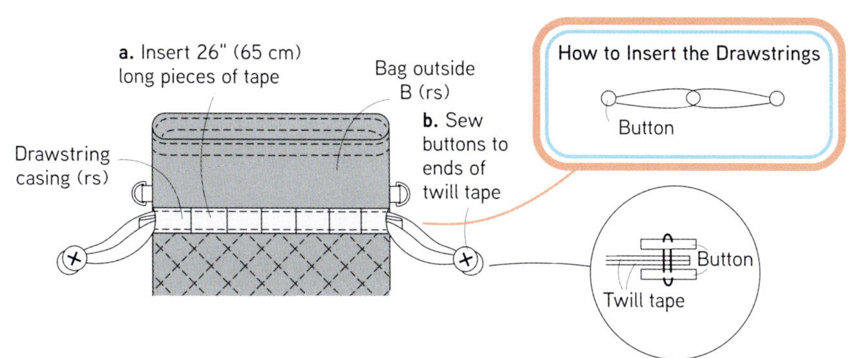

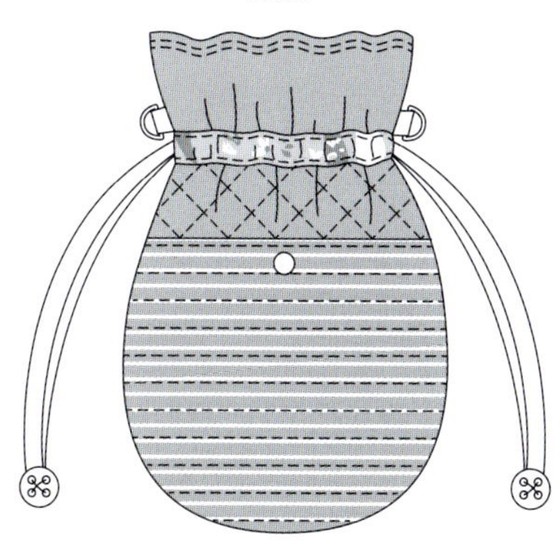

Finished Diagrams

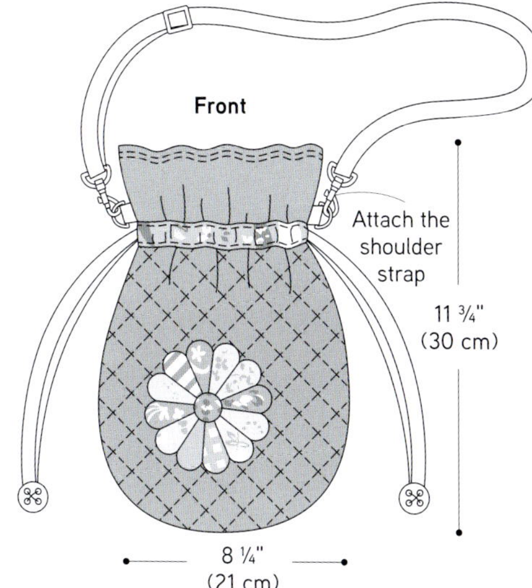

Scrappy Patchwork *Pouch*

This lovely round drawstring pouch is made with six different print fabrics to achieve a classic scrappy look. The bag's round shape makes it fun to use and pretty to look at. Covered button tabs add a cute finishing touch.

When opened, this pouch stands up on its own, making it convenient for taking small items in and out.

Designed by: Sentir le vent (Kazuyo Tsurumi)

MATERIALS

- **Patchwork fabric:** 4" x 8" (10 x 20 cm) scraps of 6 different prints
- **Lining fabric:** 24" x 8" (60 x 20 cm)
- **Drawstring casing fabric:** 20" x 4" (50 x 10 cm)
- **Covered button fabric:** 8" x 2" (20 x 5 cm)
- **Fusible interfacing:** 24" x 12" (60 x 30 cm)
- **Tape:** 47 1/4" (120 cm) of 3/8" (8 mm) wide twill tape
- Four 3/4" (2 cm) diameter cover buttons

Sew using 3/8" (1 cm) seam allowance, unless otherwise noted.

CUTTING INSTRUCTIONS

Trace the templates on Pattern Sheet D. Cut out the following:

Patchwork fabric:

- 6 patchwork pieces

Lining fabric:

- 6 patchwork pieces

Fusible interfacing:

- 12 patchwork pieces

Covered button fabric:

- 4 buttons

Cut out the following pieces, which do not have templates, according to the dimensions listed below. These measurements include seam allowance.

Drawstring casing fabric:

- **Drawstring casings (cut 2):** 8 3/4" x 2 3/4" (22.5 x 7 cm)

CONSTRUCTION STEPS

1. Sew the patchwork pieces together to make one pouch outside and one lining

a. Adhere fusible interfacing to the wrong side of each patchwork piece.

b. Align two patchwork pieces with right sides together. Sew together along one curved edge.

c. Press the seam to one side.

d. Follow the same process to attach a third patchwork piece and press the seam to one side.

e. Repeat steps b-d to make another set of three patchwork pieces.

f. Align the two sets with right sides together. Sew together around the curve.

g. Press the seam to one side. This will be the pouch outside.

h. Repeat steps a-g to make the lining.

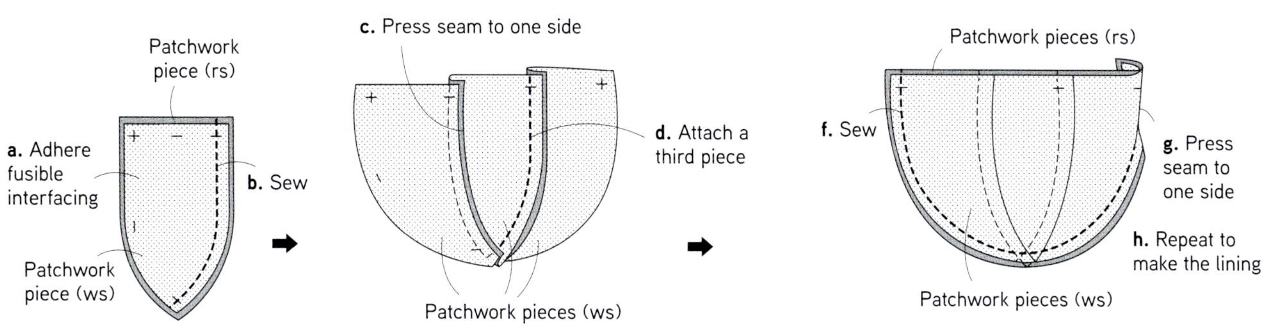

Sew the pouch outside and lining together

a. Insert the lining into the pouch outside with wrong sides together.

b. Baste together around the top using ¼" (5 mm) seam allowance.

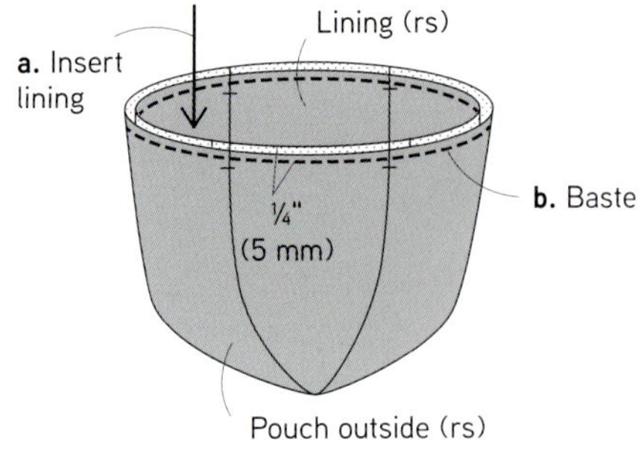

Make the drawstring casing

a. Align the two drawstring casings with right sides together. Sew together along the short ends, starting at the edge of the fabric, sewing for ⅜" (1 cm), leaving a 1" (2.5 cm) opening, and then sewing to the other edge.

b. Press the seams open.

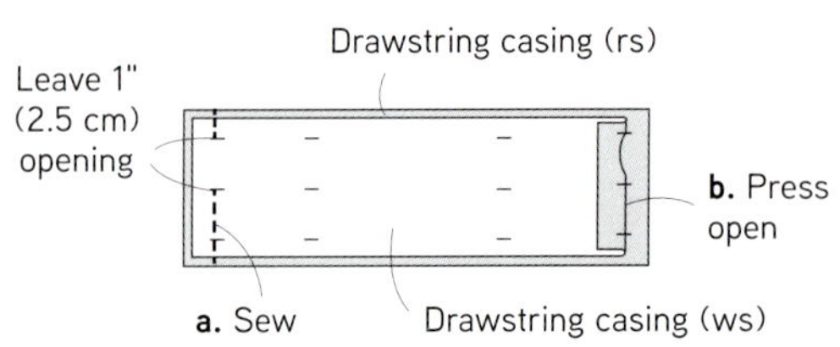

4. Attach the drawstring casing

a. Fold and press the lower raw edge of the drawstring casing over ⅜" (1 cm) to the wrong side. This is the edge farthest from the openings.

b. Align the drawstring casing and pouch outside with right sides together. Sew together around the top of the pouch.

c. Fold the drawstring casing up so the right side is facing out. Press the seam toward the drawstring casing.

d. Edgestitch the drawstring casing, stitching 1/16" (2 mm) from the seam.

e. Fold the drawstring casing in half, bringing it to the inside of the pouch.

f. Hand stitch the drawstring casing to the lining.

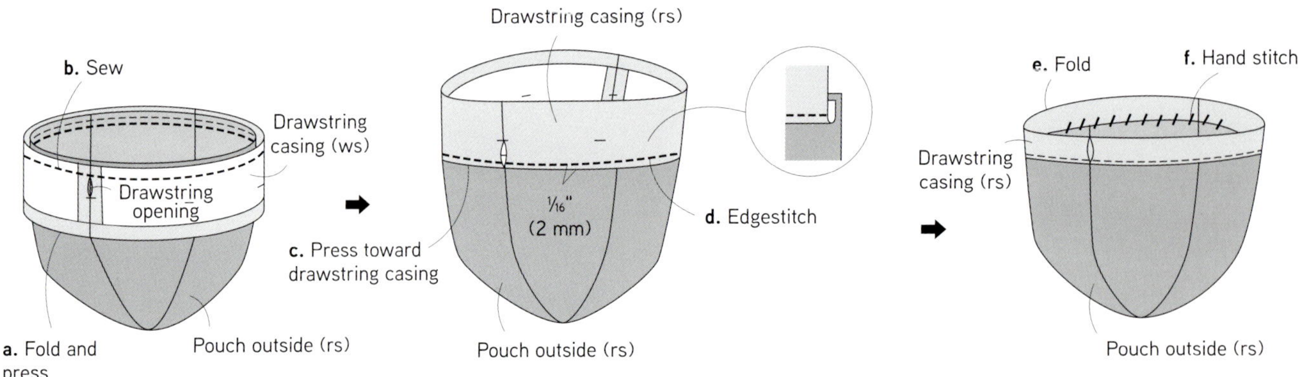

5. Make the covered buttons

a. Baste around the button fabric using ¼" (5 mm) seam allowance. Leave long thread tails.

b. Place a cover button on the wrong side of the fabric.

c. Pull the thread tails to gather the fabric around the button. Knot to secure the fabric in place.

d. Repeat steps a-c to make a total of four covered buttons.

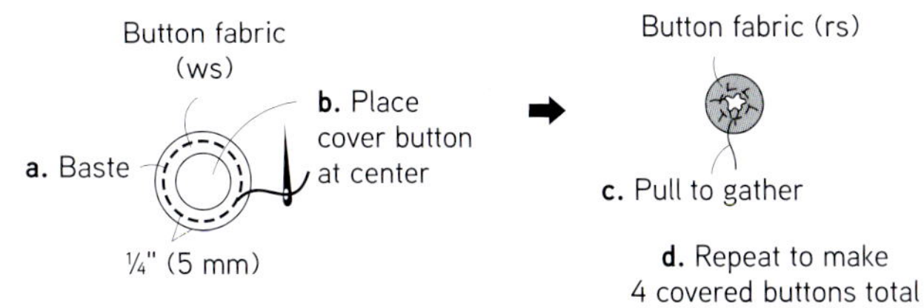

6. Insert the drawstrings

a. Pass a 24" (60 cm) long piece of tape through the casing using one of the drawstring openings. Repeat, inserting another 24" (60 cm) long piece of tape through the other drawstring opening in the opposite direction.

b. Sandwich corresponding tape ends between two covered buttons, aligning the tape ends on top of each other. Hand sew the covered buttons together, stitching through the tape to secure it in place.

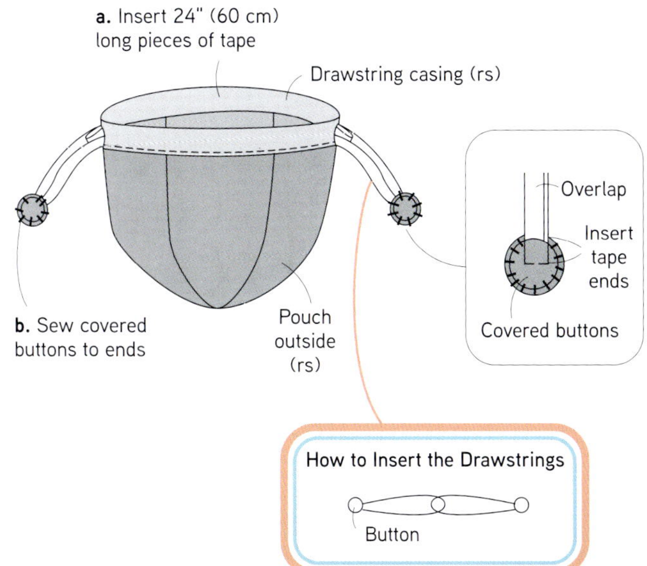

Finished Diagram

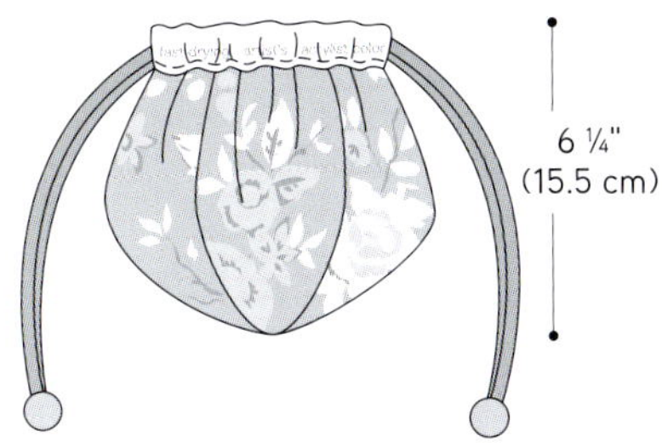

Circle *Pouch*

This cute circle-shaped pouch is convenient for storing makeup and other cosmetic items. When you untie the drawstring, the bag opens wide, allowing you to quickly find what you need inside.

Position everything you want to store inside the bag. → Pull the left and right drawstrings taut, and then tie them together. → Snap the flap shut.

MATERIALS

- **Outside fabric:** 2/3 yard
- **Lining fabric:** One fat quarter
- **Fusible interfacing:** 12" x 8" (30 x 20 cm)
- **Piping:** 18" (45 cm) of 3/8" (1 cm) wide piping
- **Cording:** 110" (280 cm) of 1/16" (2 mm) diameter waxed cotton cord
- One 3/4" (1.7 cm) diameter snap set

Sew using 3/8" (1 cm) seam allowance, unless otherwise noted.

CUTTING INSTRUCTIONS

Trace the templates on Pattern Sheet D. Cut out the following:

Outside fabric:

- 1 pouch outside
- 2 flaps

Lining fabric:

- 1 pouch lining

Fusible interfacing:

- 2 flaps

Cut out the following pieces, which do not have templates, according to the dimensions listed below. These measurements include seam allowance.

Outside fabric:

- **Drawstring casings (cut 2):** 24 1/2" x 2" (62.5 x 5 cm)

CONSTRUCTION STEPS

1. Make the drawstring casings

a. Fold and press the seam allowance to the wrong side on the short ends of one drawstring casing.

b. Edgestitch in place, stitching 1/16" (2 mm) from the fold.

c. Fold the drawstring casing in half with right sides facing out.

d. Baste the two layers of fabric together along the long edge, positioning one row of stitching 1/8" (3 mm) from the edge and the other 1/16" (2 mm) away from that. Leave long thread tails.

e. Repeat steps a-e to make another drawstring casing.

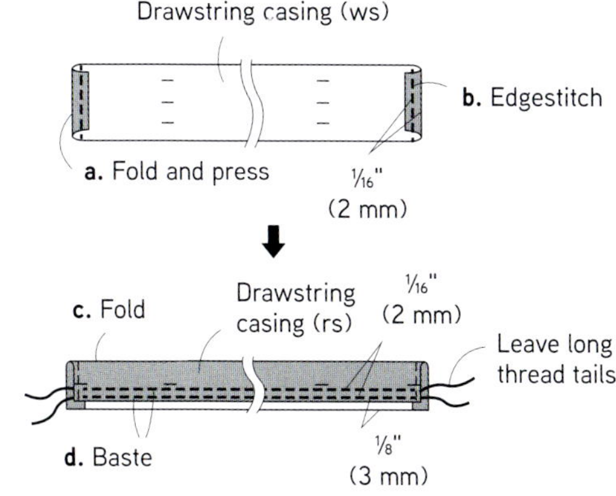

2. Sew the drawstring casings to the pouch outside

a. Align the drawstring casings with the right side of the pouch outside, matching up the centers and ends as noted on the templates. Make sure the folded edges of the casings face the inside of the circle.

b. Pull the thread tails on the drawstring casings to gather the fabric until the size matches the pouch outside.

c. Press with an iron to prevent wrinkles and pin in place.

d. Baste the drawstring casings in place, using a scant 3/8" (8 mm) seam allowance.

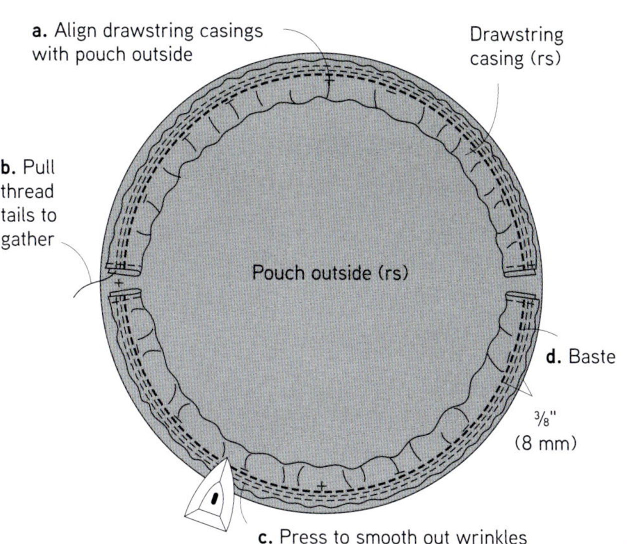

3. Sew the pouch outside and lining together

a. Align the pouch outside and lining with right sides together. Sew together around the circle, leaving a 2 3/4" (7 cm) opening.

b. Make clips into the seam allowance around the entire circle.

c. Press the seam open.

d. Turn right side out through the opening.

e. Fold the opening seam allowance in. Topstitch the pouch outside, stitching 1/16" (2 mm) away from the edge. This process will also sew the opening closed.

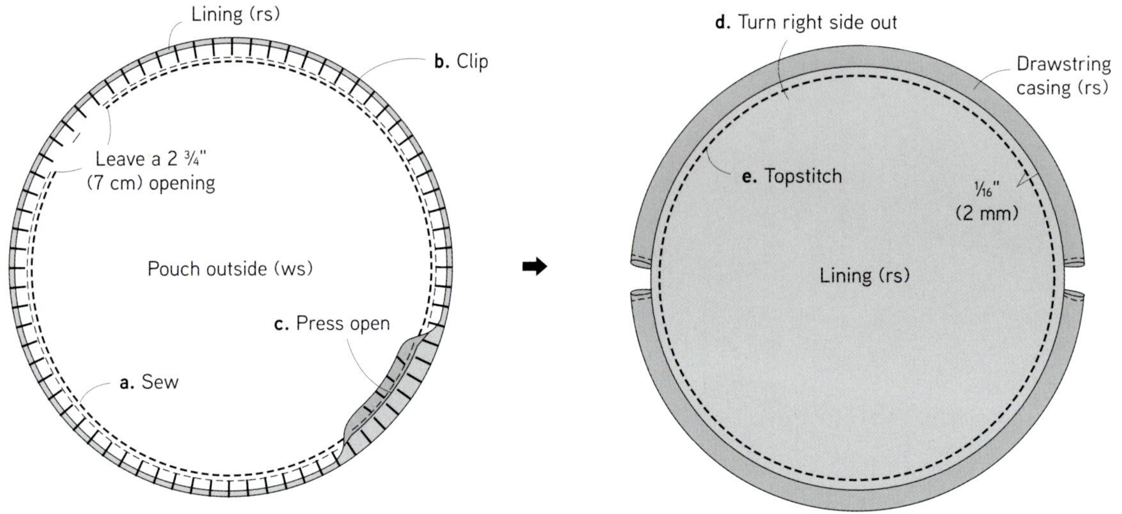

4. Make the flap

a. Adhere fusible interfacing to the wrong side of both flap pieces.

b. Make a template of the flap (do not include seam allowance). Align the template with the right side of one flap cut from fabric (this will be the flap front). Use an iron to press the piping around the outline of the template and pin in place. **Note:** The piping will start and stop just short of the seam allowance on the straight edge of the flap.

c. Baste the piping to the flap front using 1/4" (5 mm) seam allowance, starting and stopping at the edge of the piping.

d. Align the flap front and flap back with right sides together. Sew together around the curved edge.

e. Make clips into the seam allowance along the curves.

f. Press the seam open.

g. Turn the flap right side out.

h. Edgestitch around the curved edge of the flap, stitching 1/16" (2 mm) from the edge.

i. Hand sew the male component of the snap to the flap back (refer to template for placement).

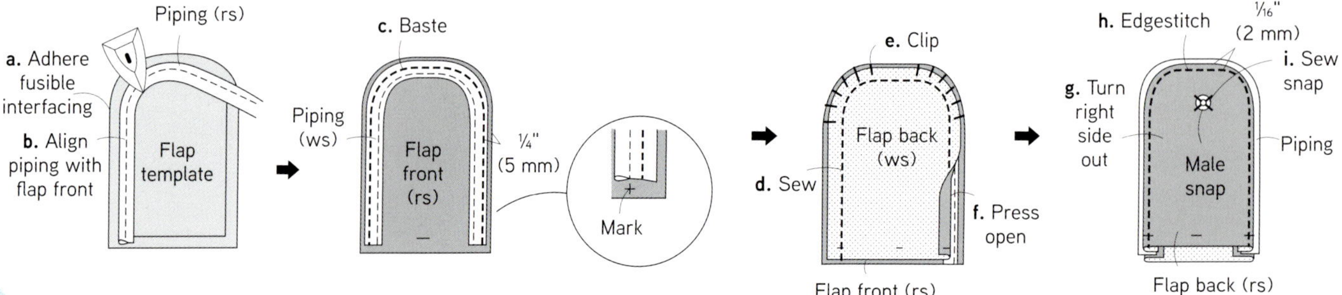

5. Sew the flap to the pouch

a. Align the flap front with the right side of the pouch outside (refer to the template for placement). Sew the flap in place by stitching across the straight edge using ¼" (6 mm) seam allowance.

b. Flip the flap up so the flap front is now facing up. Topstitch the flap in place using a scant ³/₈" (8 mm) seam allowance.

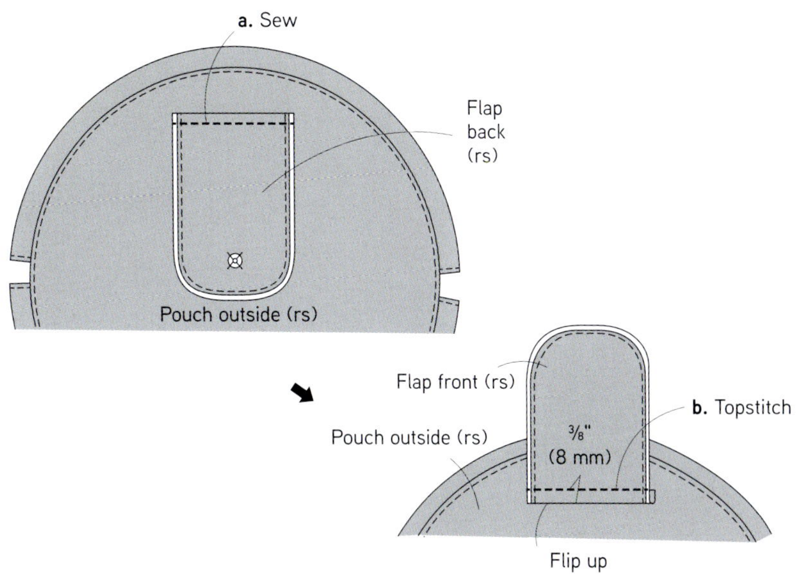

6. Insert the drawstrings

a. Hand sew the female component of the snap to the pouch outside (refer to template for placement).

b. Pass a 55" (140 cm) long piece of cord through each drawstring casing.

c. Tie the corresponding cord ends together in a knot.

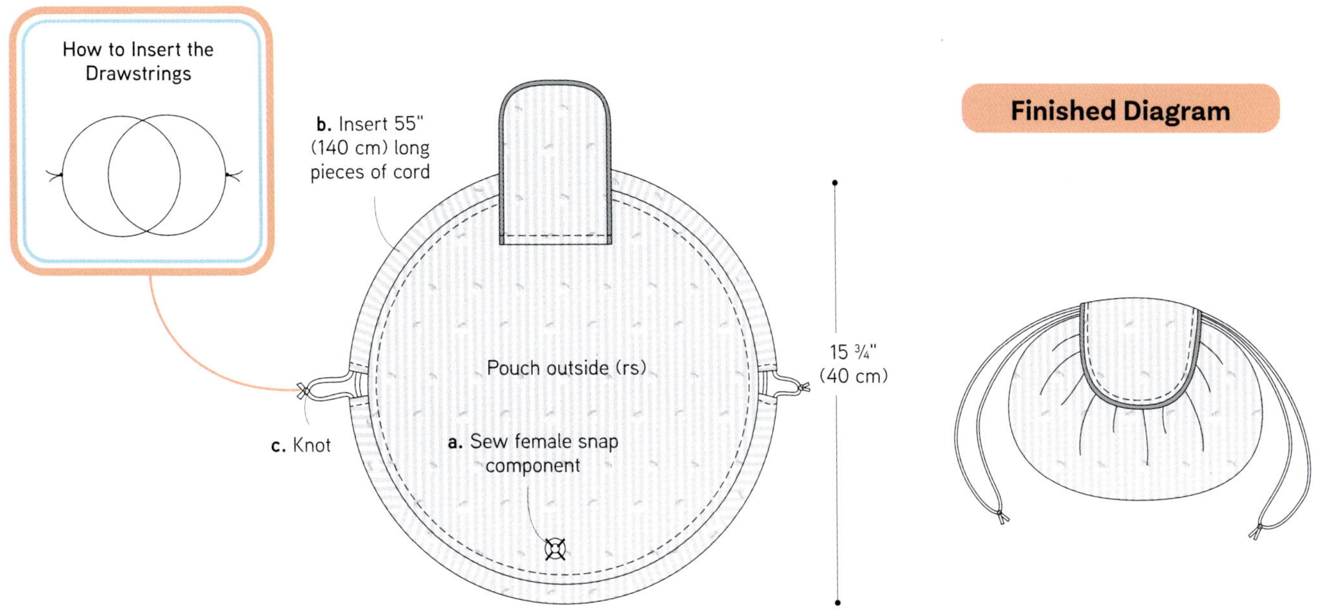

Everyday Shoulder Bag

This compact bag is perfect for both special occasions and everyday use. A drawstring closure gives the bag a pretty shape, while the adjustable strap makes it functional and comfortable to wear.

MATERIALS

- **Outside fabric:** 1/2 yard
- **Lining fabric:** One fat quarter
- **Cording:** 3 1/4 yards (2.9 m) of 1/4" (4 mm) diameter waxed cotton cord

CUTTING INSTRUCTIONS

Trace the templates on Pattern Sheet C. Cut out the following:

Outside fabric:

- 2 bag outside A
- 1 bag outside B
- 2 tabs

Lining fabric:

- 1 lining

Sew using 3/8" (1 cm) seam allowance, unless otherwise noted.

CONSTRUCTION STEPS

1. Attach the loop and strap

a. Cut a 2 1/2" (6.6 cm) long piece of waxed cotton cord and fold it into a loop. Baste to one bag outside A piece following the placement noted on the template. Use 1/4" (5 mm) seam allowance when basting.

b. Cut a 47 1/4" (120 cm) long piece of waxed cotton cord and baste to the same bag outside A piece following the placement noted on the template. Use 1/4" (5 mm) seam allowance when basting.

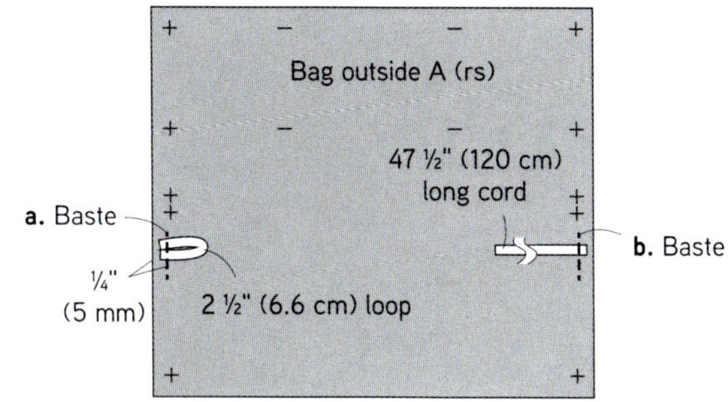

2. Assemble the bag outside

a. With right sides together, sew one bag outside A to the top edge of bag outside B and one to the bottom edge. Make sure to align the correct edge of bag outside A with bag outside B as noted on the template.

b. Press the seam allowances toward bag outside B.

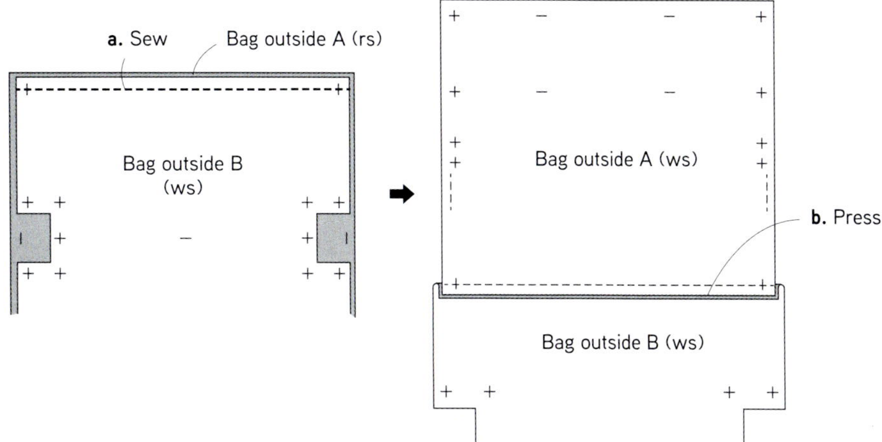

3. Sew the bag outside and lining together

a. Align the assembled bag outside from step 2 and the lining with right sides together. Sew together along the top and bottom edges.

b. Press the seam allowances open.

c. Next, separate the two layers and fold both the lining and bag outside B in half along the center bottom.

d. Following the line marked on the template, fold each bag outside A piece to create a 2 ¾" (7 cm) section above the lining. This will become the area above the drawstring casing at the top of the bag.

e. Sew the bag together along the left and right edges, avoiding the folded sections from step d. Make sure to leave a 4" (10 cm) opening in the lining. This will be used to turn the bag right side out. Always backstitch when starting and stopping sewing for this step.

f. Next, sew along the edges of the folded sections from step d. Make sure to leave a ¾" (2 cm) opening on each side for the drawstrings for 2" (5 cm) as measured from the fold.

g. Press the seam open.

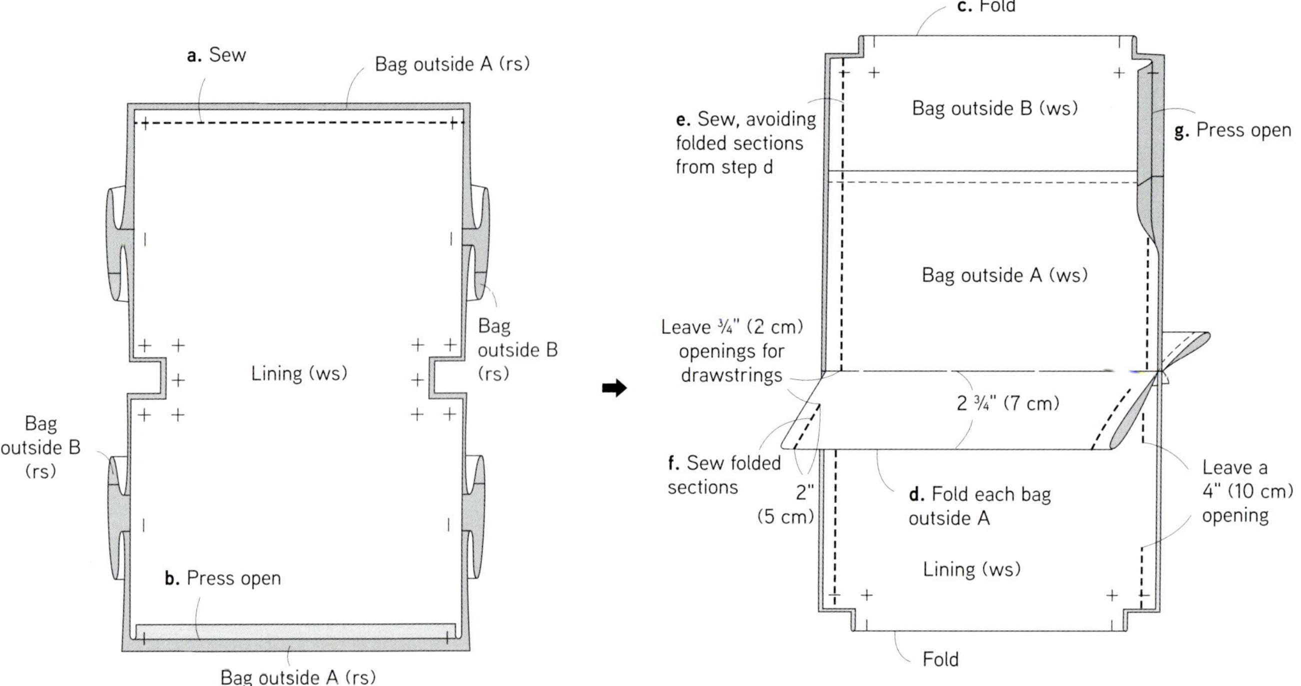

4. Miter the corners

a. On the bag outside, align each side seam with the bottom fold.

b. Sew a 1 ¼" (3 cm) long seam to miter each corner.

c. Follow the same process to miter the corners on the lining.

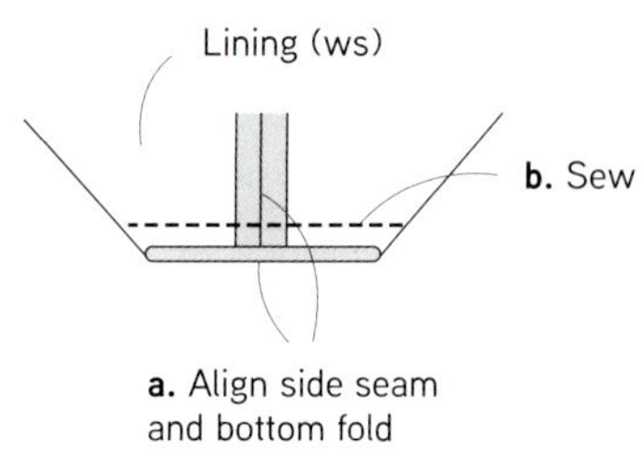

c. Repeat to miter corners on lining

5. Make the drawstring casing

a. Turn the bag right side out, but leave the lining separate from the bag outside.

b. Hand stitch the opening closed.

c. Tuck the bag outside inside the lining.

d. Next, topstitch to secure the folded section from step 3d in place on the inside of the bag. Stitch just above where this section meets the lining.

e. Topstitch another row of stitching 3/4" (2 cm) above the row sewn in step 5d. This should be about 2" (5 cm) from the top of the bag.

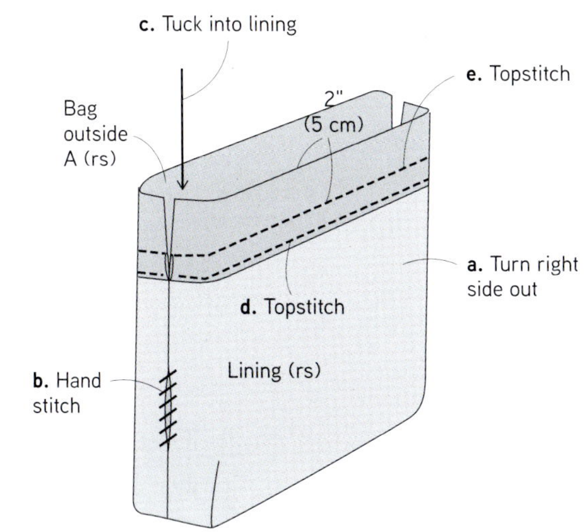

6. Insert the drawstrings

a. Pass a 31 1/2" (80 cm) long piece of cord through the casing using one of the drawstring openings.

b. Repeat step a, inserting the cord through the other drawstring opening in the opposite direction.

c. To make the tabs, fold and press the seam allowance to the wrong side on the top and bottom edges.

d. Fold each tab in half with right sides together.

e. Sew together along the left and right edges.

f. Turn right side out.

g. Insert the two cord ends into each tab so the length of cord inside the tab measures about 3/8" (1 cm).

h. Hand stitch the tab closed, securing the cord ends inside.

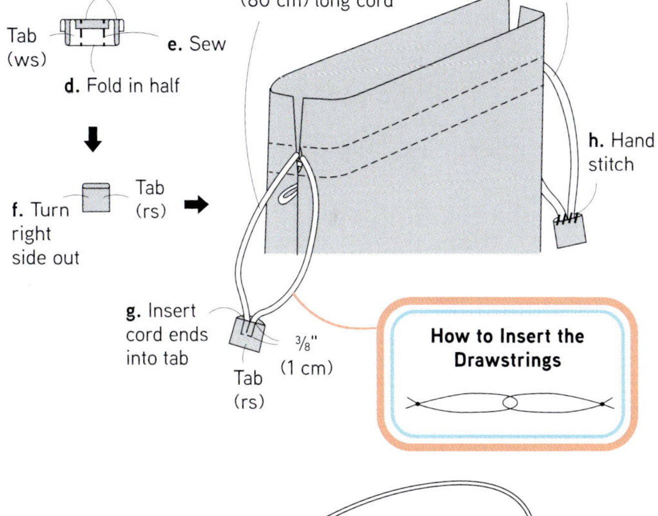

7. Finish the bag

a. Thread the shoulder strap through the loop from step 1.

b. Tie an adjustable knot as shown below. This will allow you to adjust the length of the shoulder strap.

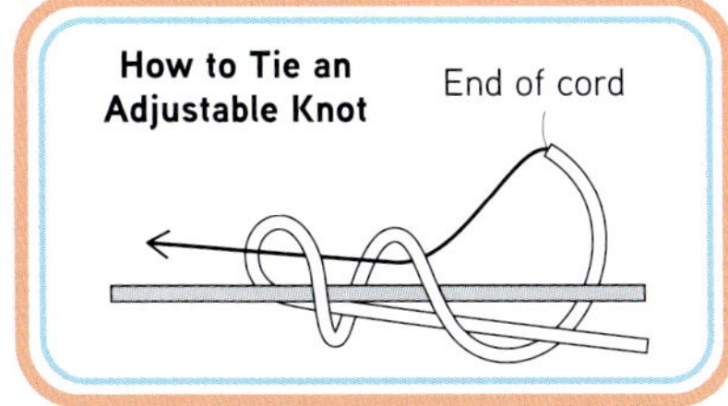

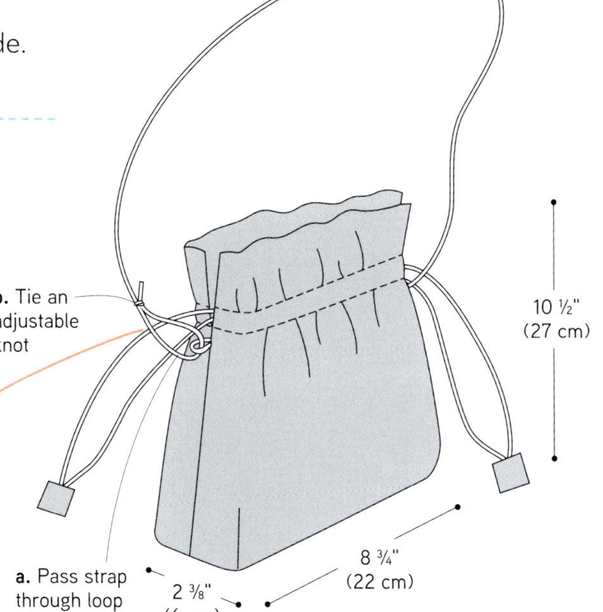

Drawstring Bucket Tote

This bucket-shaped tote bag is a perfect opportunity to pair complementary fabrics together—use one fabric for the outside and a coordinating print for the drawstring closure. Opt for a structured canvas fabric to give the bag a beautiful silhouette.

The drawstring closure allows you to store a lot inside this bag. And as an added bonus, you don't have to worry about anything falling out or being visible.

MATERIALS

- **Outside fabric:** 2/3 yard
- **Drawstring casing/lining fabric:** 1 yard
- **Heavyweight fusible interfacing:** 30" x 20" (76 x 51 cm)
- **Cording:** 82" (210 cm) of 1/8" (3 mm) diameter cord
- One pair of 16" (40 cm) handles

CUTTING INSTRUCTIONS

Trace the templates on Pattern Sheet D. Cut out the following:

Outside fabric:

- 2 bag outsides
- 1 bottom

Heavyweight fusible interfacing:

- 2 bag outsides
- 1 bottom

Drawstring casing/ lining fabric:

- 2 bag linings
- 1 bottom lining

Cut out the following pieces, which do not have templates, according to the dimensions listed below. These measurements include seam allowance.

Drawstring casing/ lining fabric:

- **Drawstring casings (cut 2):** 17 3/4" x 9 5/8" (45.1 x 24 cm)

Sew using 3/8" (1 cm) seam allowance, unless otherwise noted.

CONSTRUCTION STEPS

1. Sew the bag outside and lining together

a. Zigzag stitch the raw edges on the short sides of each drawstring casing piece individually.

b. Align the two drawstring casing pieces with right sides together. Sew together along the shorter sides, starting 3 1/8" (8 cm) from the top raw edge.

c. Press the seams open.

d. Fold and press the seam allowance over 3/8" (1 cm) to the wrong side above the starting points from step b. Topstitch in place using 1/4" (5 mm) seam allowance.

e. Fold and press the top raw edge over 3/8" (1 cm) to the wrong side. Then, fold and press over another 3/4" (2 cm). Topstitch in place using a scant 3/4" (1.8 cm) seam allowance.

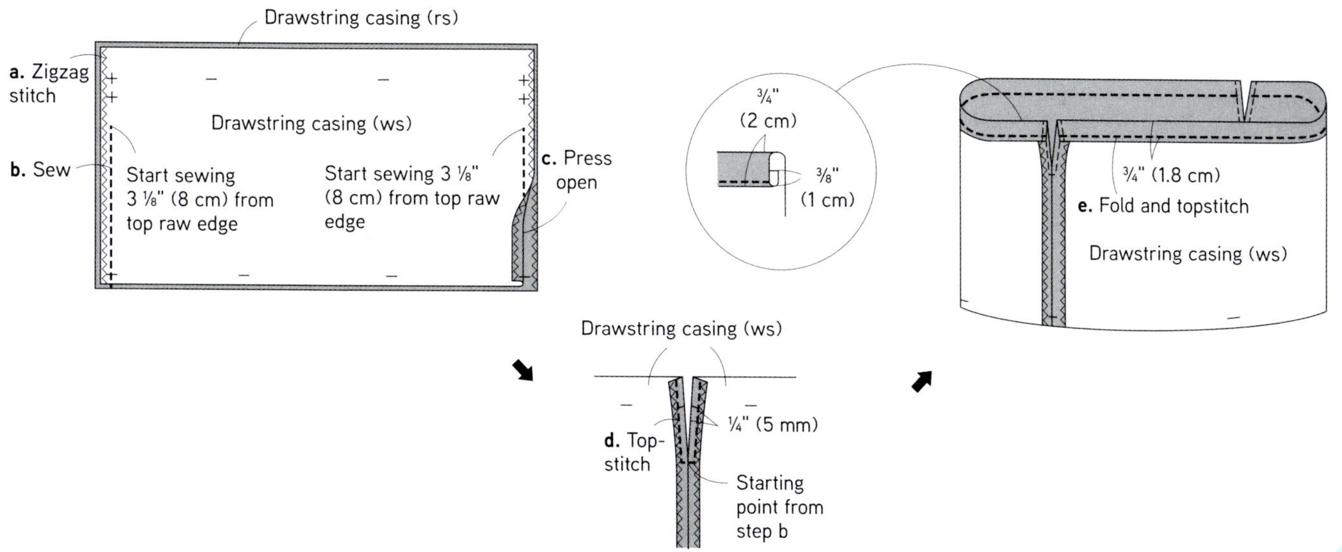

2. Sew the bag outside

a. Adhere fusible interfacing to the wrong side of each bag outside piece.

b. Align the two bag outside pieces with right sides together. Sew together along the sides, starting at the top raw edge and stopping at the bottom seam allowance mark.

c. Press the seam open.

d. Repeat steps b-c for the lining.

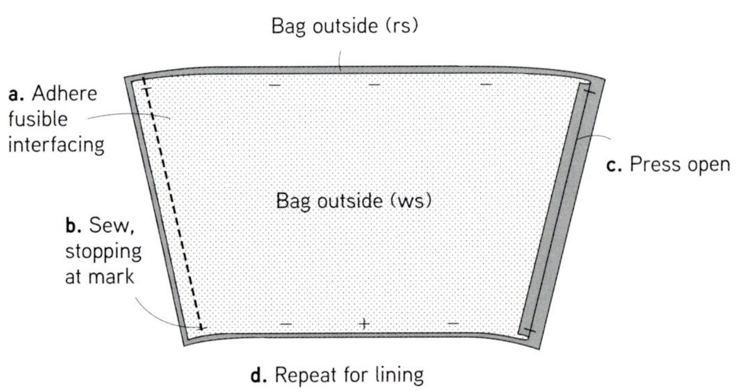

3. Attach the bottom

a. Adhere fusible interfacing to the wrong side of the bag bottom.

b. Align the bag outside and bottom with right sides together. Match up the centers and sides, adjusting the areas of the side seam allowances left unsewn in step 2b to make the bag outside fit the bottom. Pin in place.

c. Pin in place around the rest of the bag bottom.

d. Baste the bottom in place using a scant ³/₈" (1 cm) seam allowance.

e. Next, sew the bottom in place using ³/₈" (1 cm) seam allowance.

f. Remove the basting stitches from step d. Make clips into the seam allowance.

g. Press the seam open.

h. Repeat steps b-g to sew the lining and bottom lining together.

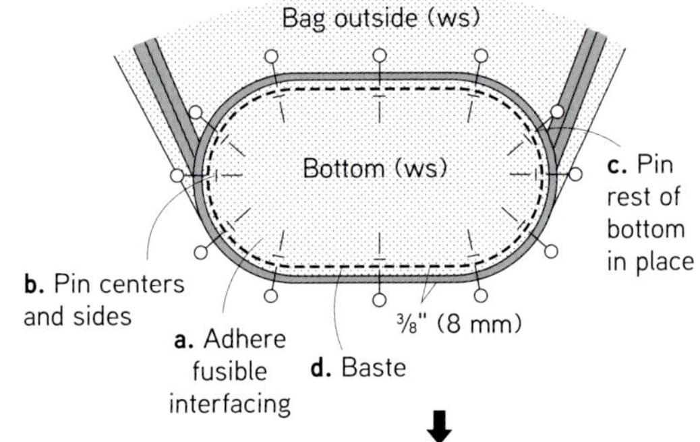

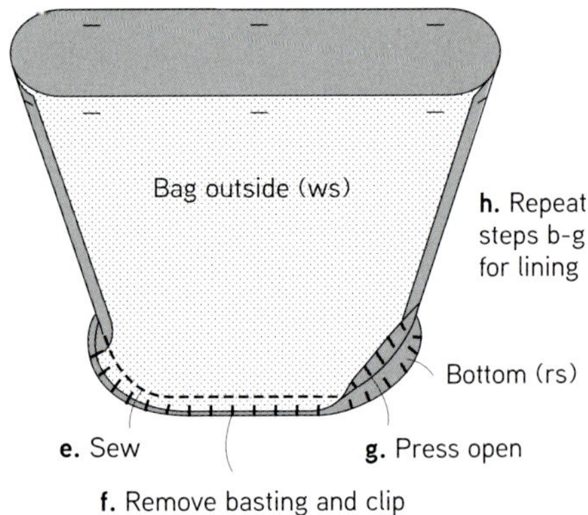

4. Assemble the bag

a. Insert the lining into the bag outside with wrong sides together.

b. Baste together around the top of the bag using ¹/₄" (5 mm) seam allowance.

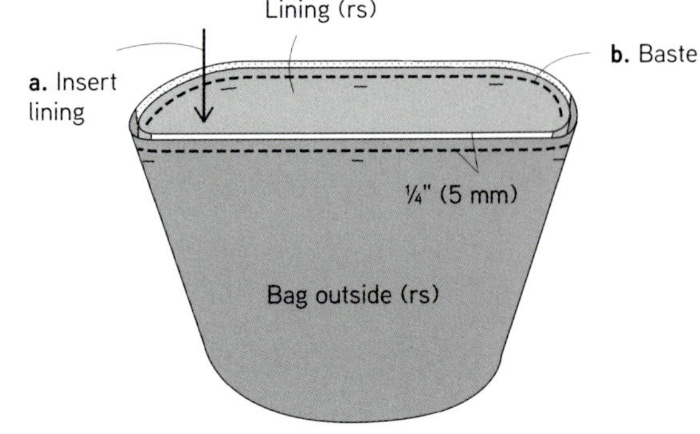

5. Attach the drawstring casings

a. Align the bag outside and drawstring casings with right sides together, matching up the side seams.

b. Sew together around the top of the bag.

c. Tuck the drawstring casing down inside the bag.

d. Topstitch two rows, stitching through all three layers of the bag outside, lining, and drawstring casings. Position one row of stitching $^1/_{16}$" (2 mm) from the top of the bag and the other row $^1/_2$" (1.2 cm) from the top of the bag.

e. Pull the drawstring casings out from the inside of the bag so they extend upward.

f. Pass a 41" (105 cm) long piece of cord through each drawstring casing.

g. Tie the corresponding cord ends together in a knot.

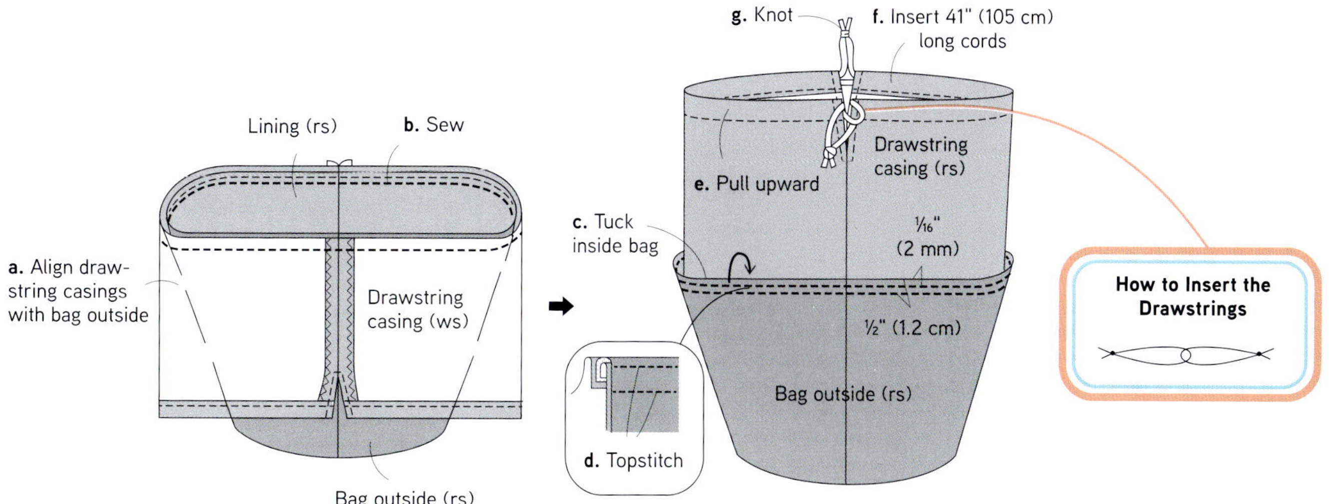

6. Finish the bag

Sew the handles to the bag outside following the placement noted on the template.

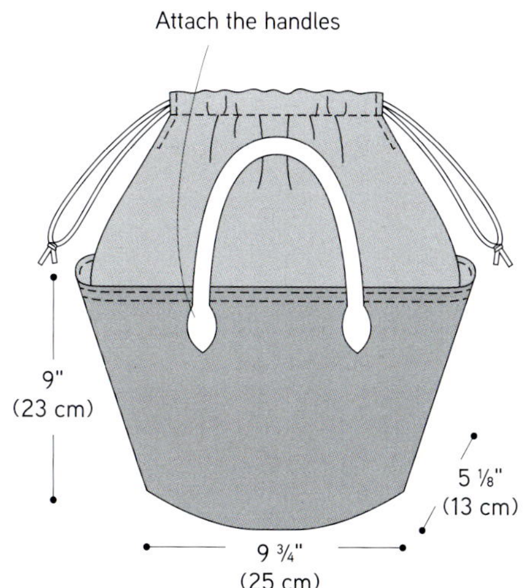

Crossbody *Sacoche*

This sporty crossbody bag is great for shopping, travel, and everyday use. It features an outside pocket, wide gusset allowing for lots of storage, and drawstring closure to keep your valuables stored safely inside.

Even though it's compact, this bag offers plenty of storage space inside.

MATERIALS

- **Outside fabric:** 3/4 yard
- **Lining fabric:** One fat quarter
- **Fusible fleece:** 24" x 32" (60 x 80 cm)
- **Cording:** 67" (170 cm) of 1/4" (7 mm) diameter cord
- Two cord locks
- Two 1" (2.5 cm) inner diameter D-rings
- 59" (150 cm) of 1" (2.5 cm) wide webbing
- Two 1" (2.5 cm) inner diameter swivel hooks
- One 1" (2.5 cm) inner diameter adjustable slider buckle

CUTTING INSTRUCTIONS

Trace the templates on Pattern Sheet B. Cut out the following:

Outside fabric:

- 2 bag outsides
- 1 pocket

Lining fabric:

- 2 bag linings

Cut out the following pieces, which do not have templates, according to the dimensions listed below. These measurements include seam allowance.

Outside fabric:

- **Outside gusset A (cut 1):** 3 1/8" x 21 1/2" (8 x 54.5 cm)
- **Outside gusset B (cut 2):** 3 1/8" x 2 3/4" (8 x 7 cm)
- **Drawstring casings (cut 2):** 9 1/2" x 3 1/8" (24 x 8 cm)

Lining fabric:

- **Gusset lining (cut 1):** 3 1/8" x 21 1/2" (8 x 54.4 cm)

Sew using 3/8" (1 cm) seam allowance, unless otherwise noted.

CONSTRUCTION STEPS

1. Make the pocket

a. Fold and press the seam allowance over 3/8" (1 cm) to the wrong side along the straight top edge. Fold and press this same edge over another 3/8" (1 cm). Topstitch to secure in place, using a scant 3/8" (8 mm) seam allowance as measured from the fold.

b. Align the pocket on top of one bag outside with right sides facing out (refer to the template for placement). Baste in place using 1/4" (5 mm) seam allowance.

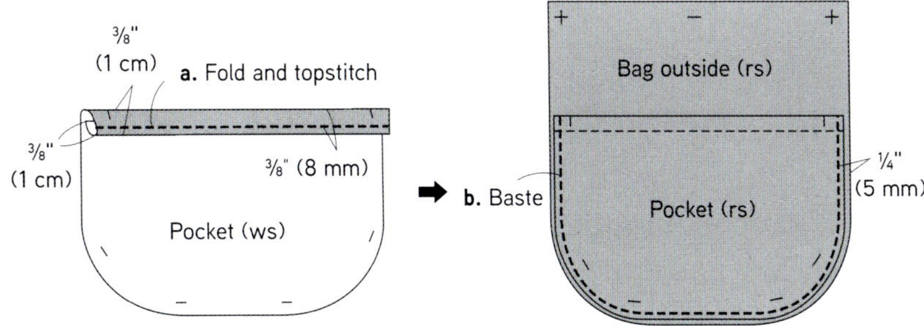

2. Make the tabs

a. Cut two 2" (5 cm) long pieces of webbing for the tabs. Thread a D-ring onto each tab and fold in half.

b. Baste one tab to the center top and one tab to the center bottom of outside gusset A, using 1/4" (5 mm) seam allowance.

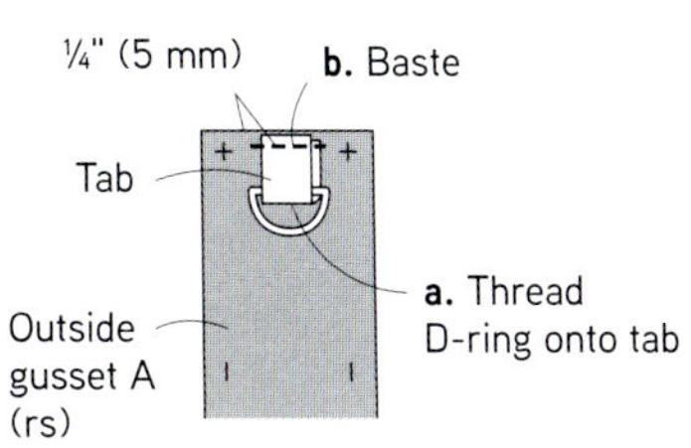

3. Make the outside gusset

a. Align each outside gusset B on top of outside gusset A with right sides together. The tabs will be sandwiched in between. Sew together along the edge.

b. Press the seam allowances toward outside gusset A.

C. Topstitch outside gusset A, stitching 1/4" (5 mm) from the seam line.

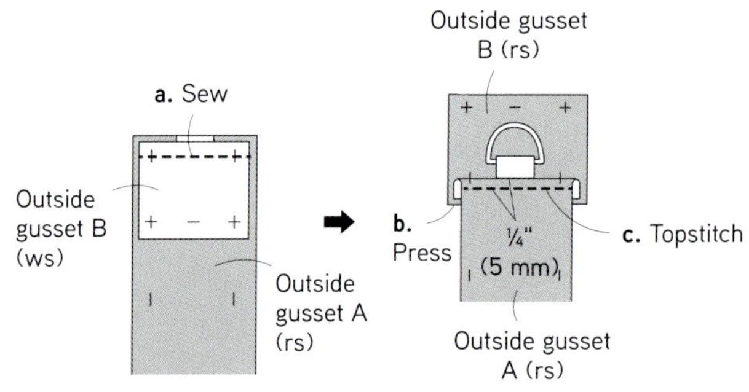

4. Sew the bag outsides and gusset together

a. With right sides together, sew the outside gusset to each bag outside.

b. Make clips into the seam allowance along the curves, being careful not to cut through the stitching line. This will help create nice smooth corners and reduce bulk.

c. Press the seam allowances open.

d. Follow the same process to sew the gusset lining to each bag lining.

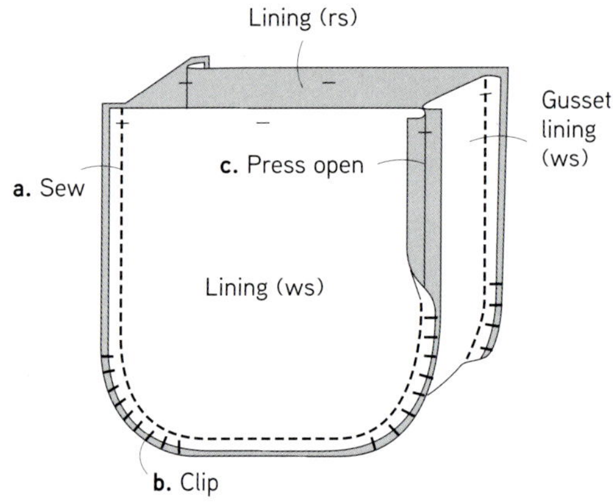

d. Repeat for lining

5. Make the drawstring casings

Fold and press the left and right edges of each drawstring casing over 1/4" (5 mm) to the wrong side. Fold and press these same edges over another 1/4" (5 mm). Edgestitch 1/8" (3 mm) from the fold.

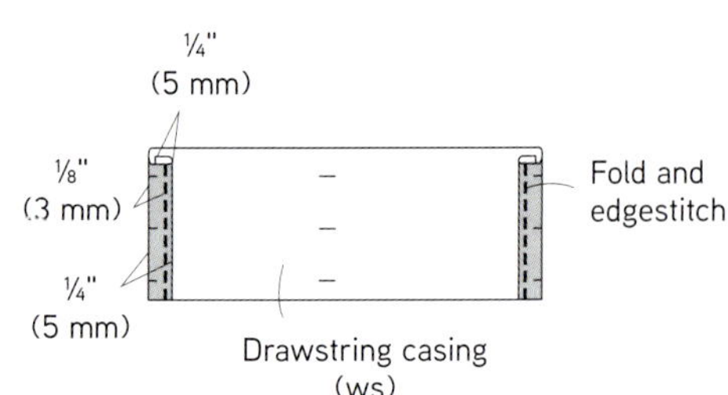

6. Attach the drawstring casings to the bag

a. Align each drawstring casing with the bag lining with right sides together. Sew together along the top edge of the bag.

b. Press the seam allowances toward the lining.

c. Fold and press the seam allowances to the wrong side on the remaining raw edges along the top of the gusset lining.

d. With right sides together, sew the remaining raw edge of each drawstring casing to a top edge of the bag outside.

e. Fold and press the seam allowances to the wrong side on the remaining raw edges along the top of the outside gusset.

f. Turn right side out.

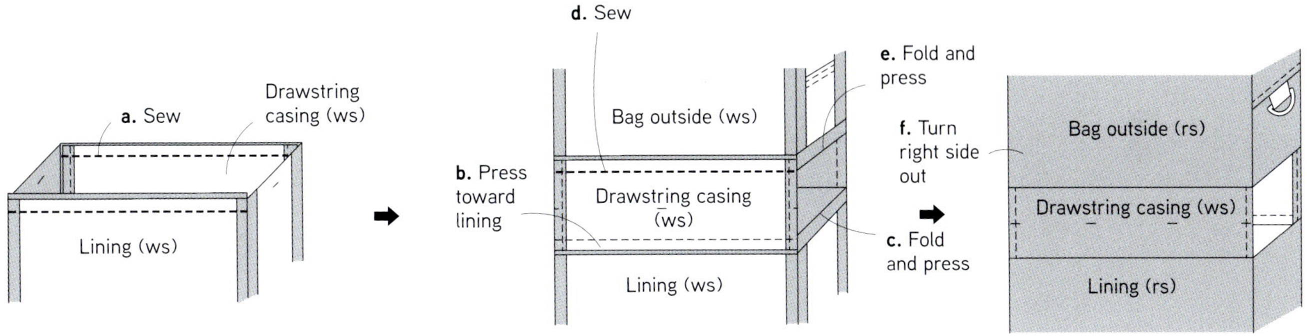

7. Insert the drawstrings

a. Tuck the lining into the bag outside.

b. Fold the drawstring casings in half, bringing them to the inside of the bag.

c. Edgestitch around the top of the bag outside, stitching 1/16" (2 mm) away from the casing seam.

d. Pass a 33 1/2" (85 cm) long piece of cord through the casings from one end of the bag.

e. Insert the cord ends through one of the cord locks.

f. Knot the cord ends together.

g. Repeat steps d-g using the remaining cord and cord lock, passing the cord through the casings from the other end of the bag.

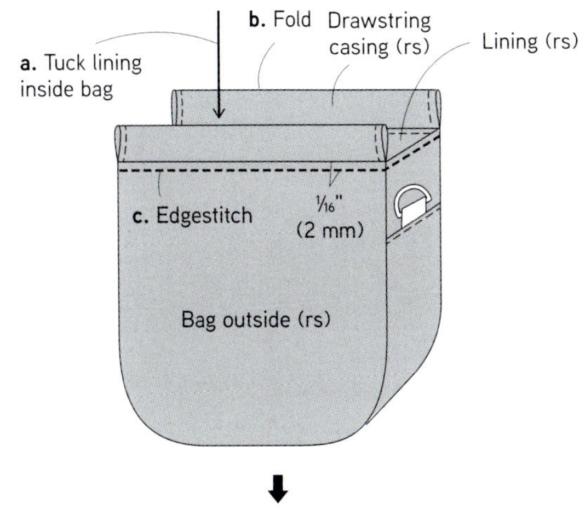

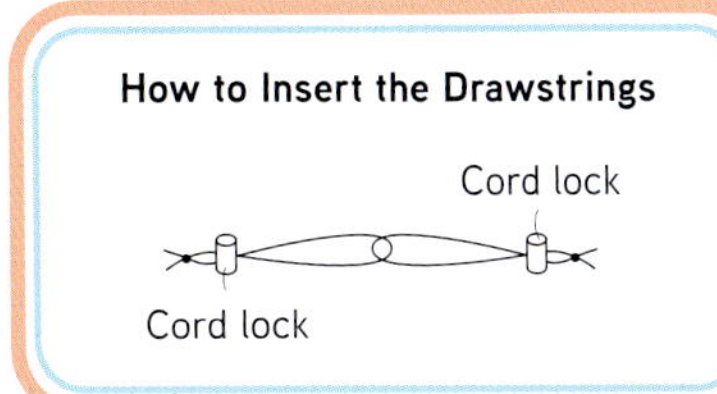

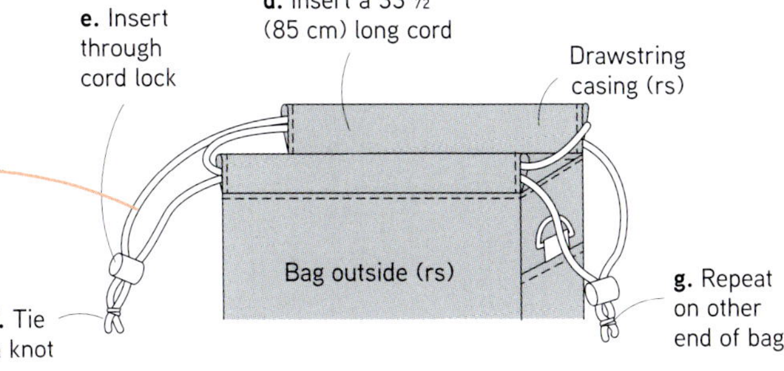

8. Make the shoulder strap

a. Thread a swivel hook onto one end of a 55" (140 cm) long piece of webbing.

b. Fold the raw edge of the webbing over ³/₈" (1 cm).

c. Adjust the swivel hook so it is positioned 1" (2.5 cm) from the folded edge of the webbing. Topstitch to secure in place, stitching through all three layers of webbing.

d. Insert the free end of the webbing through an adjustable slider buckle. The webbing should go under the outside bars and over the center bar.

e. Thread the remaining swivel hook onto the free end of the webbing.

f. Insert the free end of the webbing back through the slider. This time, the webbing should go under the outer bar, back over the same bar, and through the half moon-shaped cut out.

g. Fold the raw edge of the webbing over ³/₈" (1 cm). Fold over another ³/₄" (2 cm). Topstitch to secure in place, stitching through all three layers of webbing.

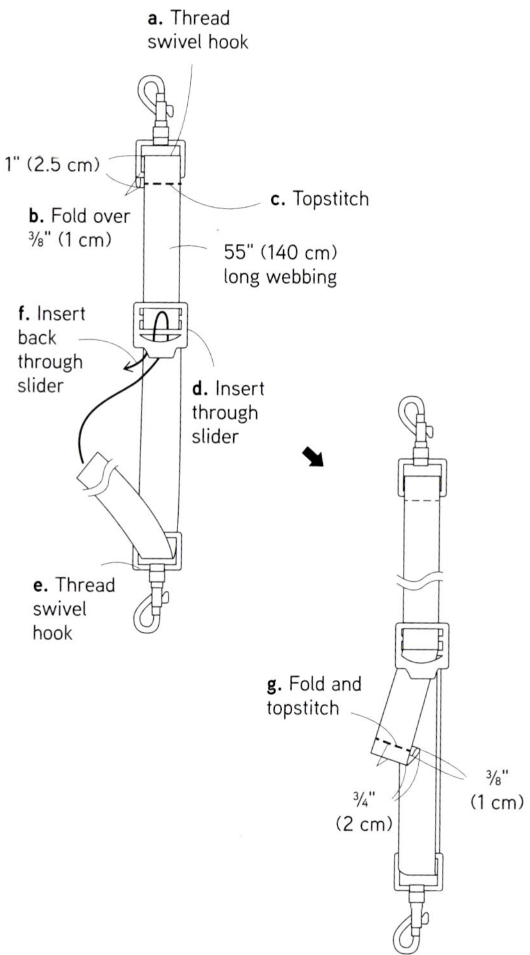

Finished Diagram

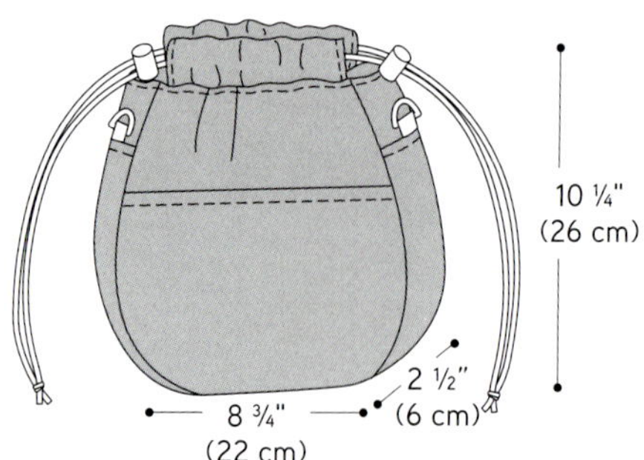

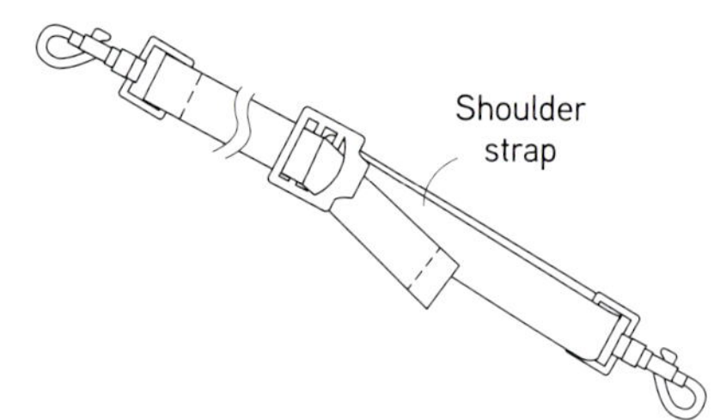

Two-Way Quilted Bag

This convertible bag is super versatile and functional. It has excellent storage capacity, so it is convenient for everyday use, as well as travel. Wear it as a crossbody bag, or remove the strap and use it as a tote—it does double duty!

You can also use this design as a tote bag—simply unclip the shoulder strap, loosen the drawstring to relax the shape of the bag, and then pull the small fabric handles to the outside.

MATERIALS

- **Outside fabric:** 2/3 yard
- **Lining fabric:** 2/3 yard
- **Fusible fleece:** 24" x 32" (60 x 80 cm)
- **Cording:** 47" (120 cm) of 1/4" (5 mm) diameter cord
- One cord lock
- Two 1/4" (5 mm) diameter cord end caps
- Two 1" (2.5 cm) inner diameter D-rings
- 55" (140 cm) of 1" (2.5 cm) wide webbing
- Two 1" (2.5 cm) inner diameter swivel hooks
- One 1" (2.5 cm) inner diameter adjustable slider buckle

Sew using 3/8" (1 cm) seam allowance, unless otherwise noted.

CUTTING INSTRUCTIONS

Trace the templates on Pattern Sheet A.
Cut out the following:

Outside fabric:
- 1 bag outside

Lining fabric:
- 1 bag lining

Fusible fleece:
- 1 bag outside

Cut out the following pieces, which do not have templates, according to the dimensions listed below. These measurements include seam allowance.

Outside fabric:
- **Handles (cut 2):** 2 3/4" x 12 3/4" (7 x 32 cm)
- **Tabs (cut 2):** 2 3/4" x 2 1/2" (7 x 6 cm)
- **Casing (cut 1):** 39 1/2" x 2 3/4" (100 x 7 cm)

Fusible fleece:
- **Handles (cut 2):** 1 3/8" x 12 3/4" (3.5 x 32 cm)

CONSTRUCTION STEPS

1. Adhere fusible fleece to the fabric pieces

Use the iron to adhere fusible fleece to the wrong side of the bag outside and both handles (refer to the diagram at right for placement).

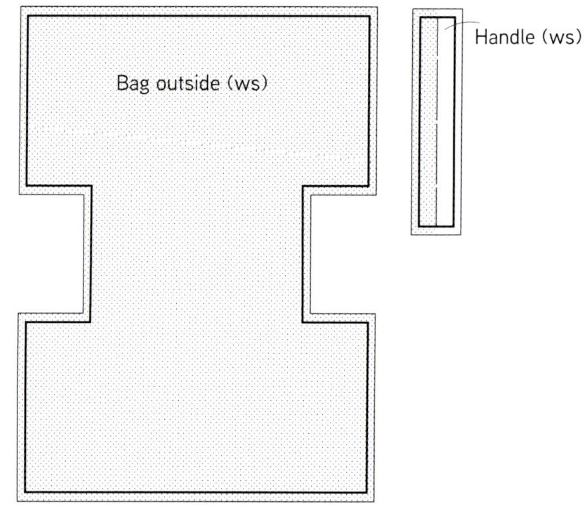

2. Quilt the bag outside

a. Draw quilting lines on the bag outside using chalk or a water-soluble pen. Position quilting lines 3/4" (2 cm) from the center line of the bag outside, then position subsequent quilting lines 1 1/2" (4 cm) apart.

b. Topstitch along the marked lines to quilt the bag outside, stitching through both the outside fabric and fusible fleece.

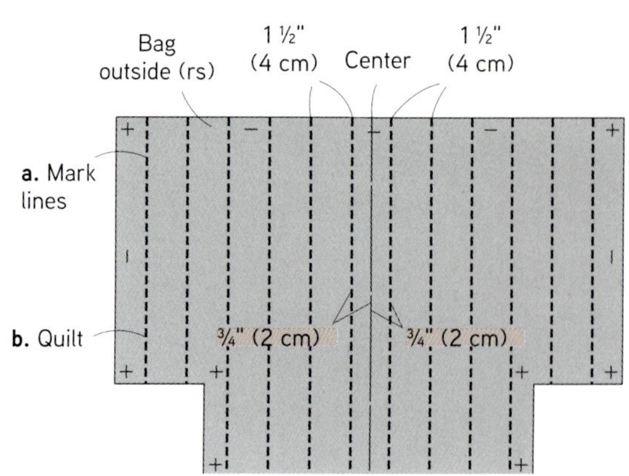

3. Make the tabs

a. Fold and press the seam allowances to the wrong side on the left and right edges of each tab.

b. Fold each tab in half, creasing along the center line. Press with the iron. Edgestitch vertical lines, stitching 1/16" (2 mm) from the left and right edges.

c. Thread a D-ring onto each tab and fold in half.

d. Baste each tab to the bag outside following placement noted on the template. Use 1/4" (5 mm) seam allowance when basting the tabs in place.

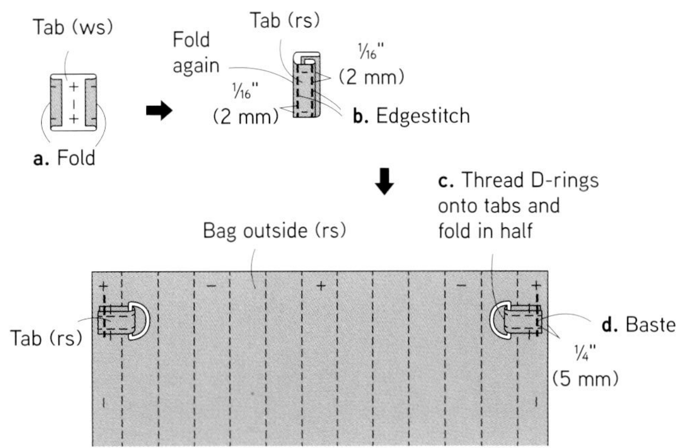

4. Sew the bag side seams

a. Fold the bag outside in half with right sides together. Sew together along the left and right edges.

b. Press the seam allowances open.

c. Follow the same process to sew the lining side seams, making sure to leave a 3" (7 cm) opening in one of the seams. This will be used to turn the bag right side out.

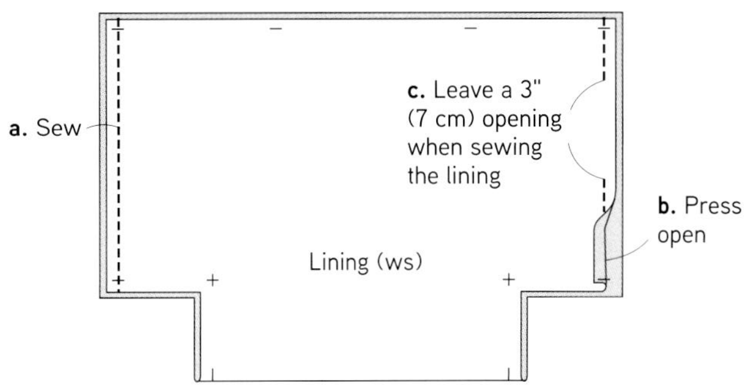

5. Miter the corners

a. On the bag outside, align each side seam with the bottom fold.

b. Sew a 3 3/4" (9.5 cm) long seam to miter each corner.

c. Follow the same process to miter the corners on the lining.

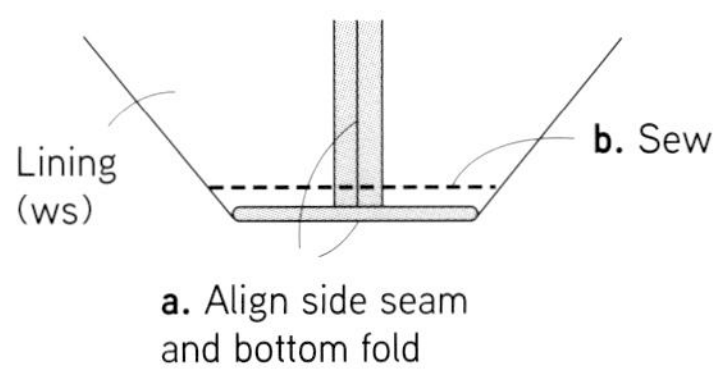

6. Make the handles

a. Fold and press the seam allowances to the wrong side on the left and right edges of each handle.

b. Fold each handle in half, creasing along the center line. Press with the iron. Edgestitch vertical lines, stitching 1/16" (2 mm) from the left and right edges.

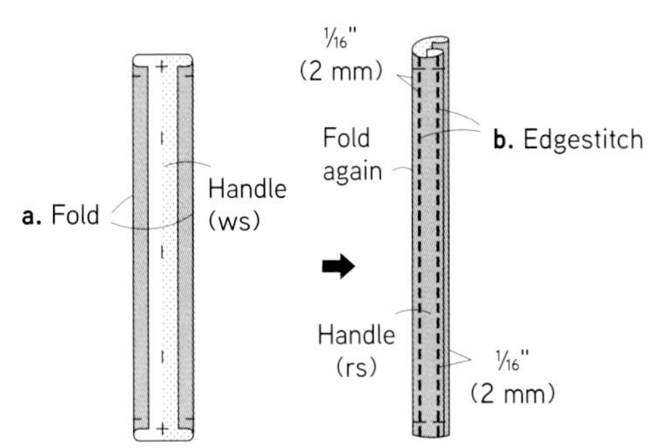

7. Make the drawstring casing

a. Fold the drawstring casing in half with right sides together. To sew together, start at the top raw edge and sew for ¼" (6 mm). Stop sewing and backstitch. Leave an opening for the drawstring, then start sewing again at the center line of the casing. Sew to bottom raw edge and backstitch.

b. Press the seam allowances open.

c. Topstitch the seam allowances in place to reinforce the drawstring opening, stitching ¼" (5 mm) from the seam line.

d. Fold the casing in half with right sides facing out, creasing along the center line.

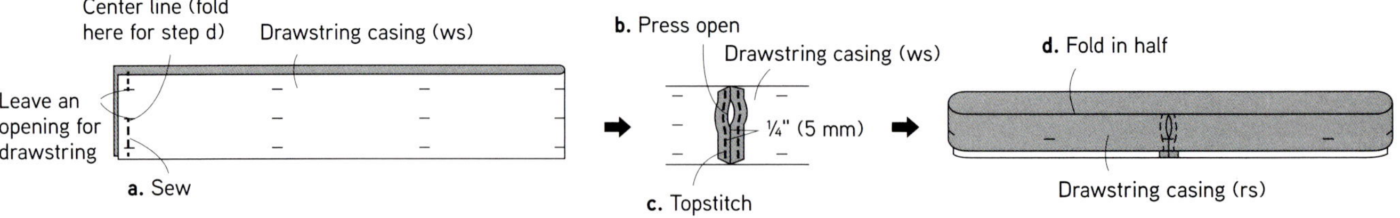

8. Attach the handles and drawstring casing

a. Align the drawstring casing and bag outside with right sides together. Make sure to position the casing so that the part with the drawstring opening is facing down against the bag outside.

b. Next, align the handles on top so that the inner edges of the handles are positioned 1¼" (3 cm) from the center line of the bag outside (refer to the template for placement).

c. Baste around the top of the bag to secure the drawstring casing and handles in place. Use a scant ⅜" (8 mm) seam allowance when basting.

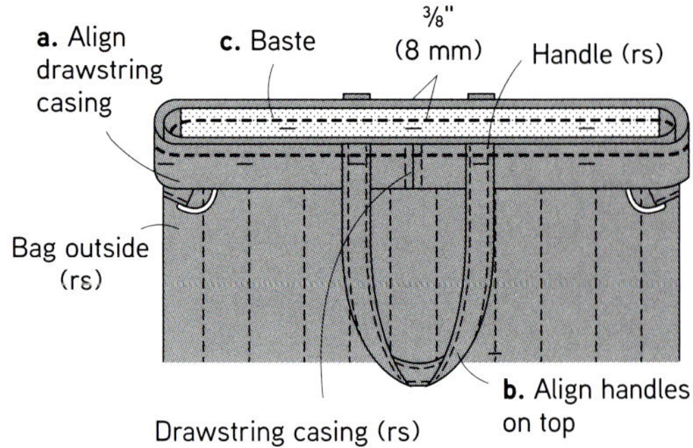

Note: The part with the drawstring opening should be facing down and aligned with the center front of the bag.

9. Sew bag outside and lining together

a. Insert the bag outside into the lining with right sides together.

b. Sew together around the top of the bag.

c. Turn right side out through the opening in the lining.

d. Hand stitch the opening closed.

e. Edgestitch the lining, stitching $\frac{1}{16}$" (2 mm) beneath the casing seam.

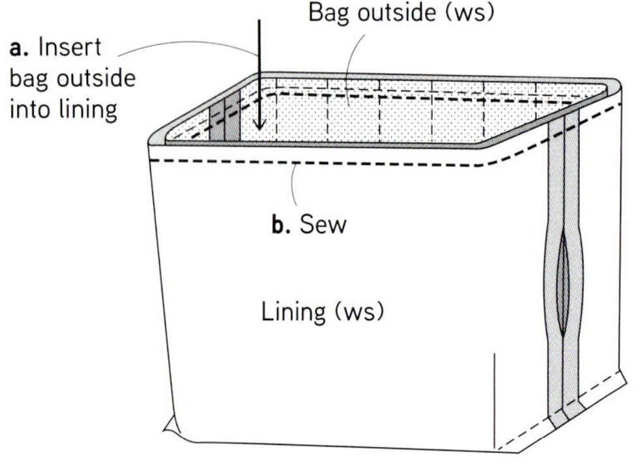

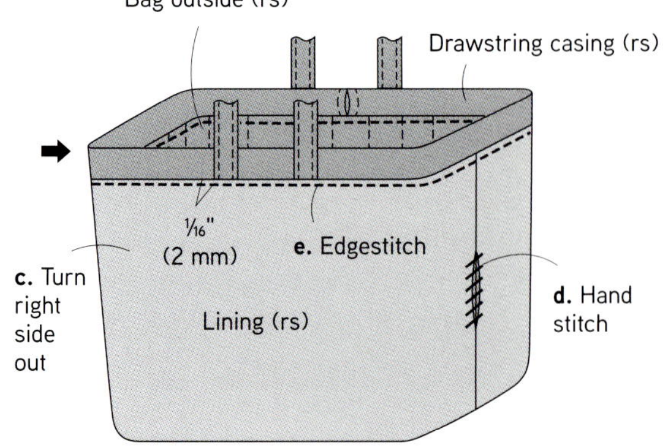

10. Make the shoulder strap

a. Insert a 55" (140 cm) long piece of webbing through the adjustable slider buckle. The webbing should go under the outside bars and over the center bar.

b. Fold the raw edge of the webbing over 3/8" (1 cm).

c. Adjust the slider so it is positioned 1 1/2" (4 cm) from the folded edge of the webbing. Topstitch to secure in place, stitching through all three layers of webbing.

d. Thread a swivel hook onto the other end of the webbing.

e. Insert the free end of the webbing back through the slider. Again, the webbing should go under the outside bars and over the center bar.

f. Thread the remaining swivel hook onto the free end of the webbing.

g. Fold the raw edge of the webbing over 3/8" (1 cm).

h. Adjust the swivel hook so it is positioned 5/8" (1.5 cm) from the folded edge of the webbing. Topstitch to secure in place, stitching through all three layers of webbing.

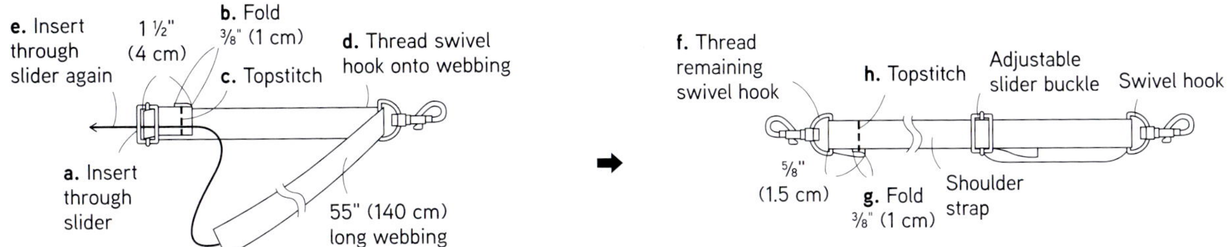

11. Insert the drawstrings

a. Pass a 47" (120 cm) long piece of cord through the casing using the drawstring opening.

b. Insert the cord ends through the cord lock.

c. Install the end caps.

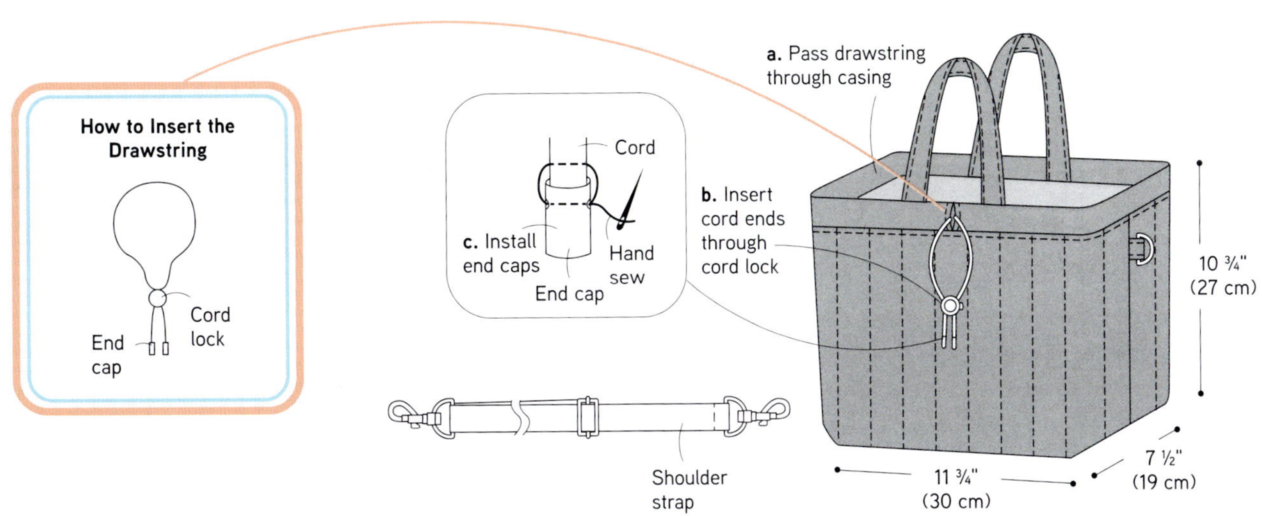

Basic Sewing Techniques for Drawstring Bags

The following guide includes some basic sewing techniques and tips that will be helpful while making drawstring bags.

HOW TO APPLY FUSIBLE INTERFACING & FUSIBLE FLEECE

Fusible Interfacing

1. Align the fusible interfacing with the wrong side of the fabric so that the adhesive side faces down. This is the side that is rough to the touch and shines when held up to the light.

2. Press with a dry iron on the medium heat setting. Use a pressing cloth or piece of paper on top of the interfacing to protect your iron from any residue transfer.

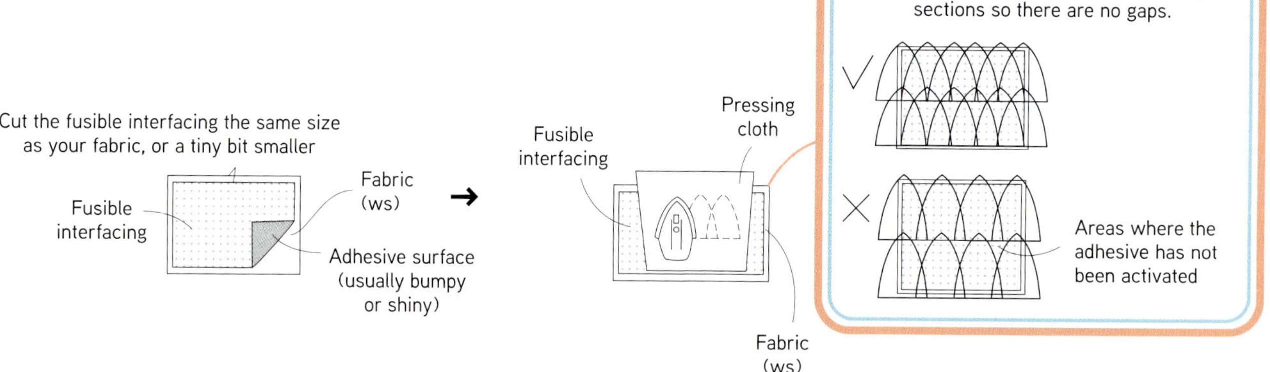

Fusible Fleece

The process for applying fusible fleece is basically the same as when applying fusible interfacing, but this time, you'll place the adhesive surface facing up and then align the fabric on top with the wrong side facing down. When ironing, be careful not to press too forcefully, as this might crush the fleece.

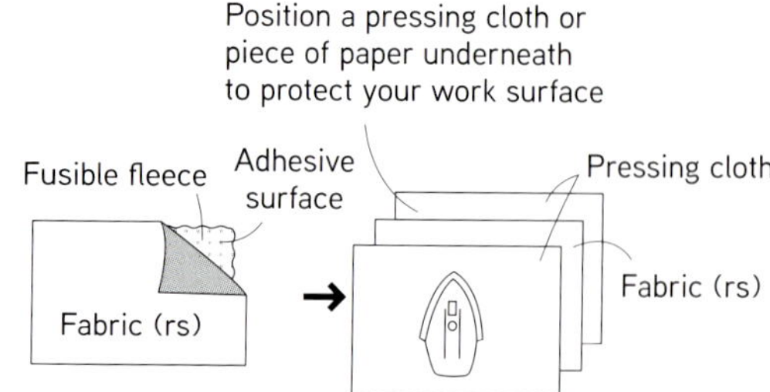